FROM GENERATION
TO GENERATION

FROM GENERATION TO GENERATION

A Memoir of Food, Family, and Identity in the Aftermath of the Shoah

Michelle Weinfeld

NEW DEGREE PRESS

FROM GENERATION TO GENERATION

A Memoir of Food, Family, and Identity in the Aftermath of the Shoah

ISBN

979-8-88504-587-2 *Paperback*

979-8-88504-932-0 *Kindle Ebook*

979-8-88504-821-7 *Digital Ebook*

In loving memory of Mike Jucowics.

Thank you for everything, Poppy.

CONTENTS

___

"Everything can be taken from a man but one thing: the last of the human freedoms—to choose one's attitude in any given set of circumstances, to choose one's own way."

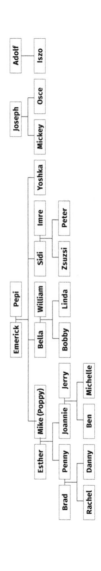

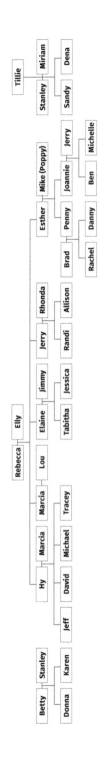

PROLOGUE

———

With cookies and rye bread in hand, my brother and I arrived at my grandparents' house. My hands clutched the bag of bread tightly, refusing to risk spilling out the contents. These weekly visits to drop off a few "essentials" became a routine to bring some semblance of normalcy back into our lives. This was my way of showing my love for them. While I was nervous, seeing my grandparents brought joy to the forefront. It overpowered the sadness present at so many of our visits.

As I walked through the door, the rush of hot air hit me. The temperature change from the crisp autumn air outside made their house border on uncomfortably warm. In September of 2020, the COVID-19 pandemic was in full swing. It was six months since the country went into lockdown and I could spend meaningful time with my grandparents. Every visit brought the fear of transmitting this new and dangerous virus without a cure. Half a year passed by, keeping them stuck inside by themselves. I couldn't sit next to them or touch them. All my visits were socially distanced and, thanks to our masks and my grandfather's hearing loss, the conversations felt like a game of telephone.

Growing up, I viewed my grandfather, Poppy, as the ultimate father figure, exemplifying strength and protection. He owned a custom furniture business and could fix anything—including his own thumb—with his handy toolkit and some duct tape. Poppy fixed problems both physical and emotional. Somehow his wisdom and compassion provided everyone he met with a sense of belonging. He created a safe space free of judgment. His advice was always coupled with quippy remarks as a reminder never to take life too seriously.

Isolation from the pandemic aged him. Arthritis made his hands curl inward like he was trying to hold onto something that long escaped his grasp. Seeing him from across the house made my heart ache in a way I had not felt before. This wasn't the same man who renovated my parents' house on his own without needing to hire a contractor. Now, he was hunched over his walker, using his forearms to hold himself up on a tray attached to the walker with duct tape for extra support. He and my grandmother were so lonely, so old. They had not had the company of our family for more than fifteen minutes at a time for the last six months. It felt like we were separated by an ocean, instead of just six feet.

Based on the Center for Disease Control (CDC) recommendations, we were limited to a fifteen-minute time slot inside. As our time came to its expiration, my brother and I walked toward the door. A heaviness thickened the air, slowing our walk and postponing our inevitable departure. Before we stepped out, Poppy called out to me.

"Just know how much I appreciate everything you do for me. I love you and I'm proud of you."

My heart sank into my stomach, my eyes began to tear, and I took one last look at him before walking out the door. Poppy never said sentimental things. I knew he loved and appreciated us, but it was an unspoken feeling hidden beneath complaints and sarcastic remarks. The affirmation, something I sometimes longed to hear, broke my heart. It was weighted with the finality of a goodbye even though I would see him next weekend.

Driving home after seeing them was difficult. My chest tightened and my breathing was shallow. I did my best to hold back tears. I constantly referred to the feeling as "nostalgia for the present." I knew I had already left "the good old days," but I still tried to make memories in the time I had left with my aging grandparents. I yearned for things to go back to the way they were before the pandemic: cooking side by side and with Poppy telling me stories of a life from long ago.

Our relationship was special, but every member of my family would say the same about their relationship with him. The most important thing to my grandfather was and will always be his family. While he was never wealthy in the traditional meaning, Poppy would say he was the richest man in the world because he had his family. After losing most of his loved ones in the Holocaust, he knew the importance of keeping the people he loved close.

Growing up, I made it a point to listen to the stories of as many Holocaust survivors as possible. The organizers of speaking events usually included a similar remark in their introduction about how hearing firsthand accounts was crucial as opportunities were fleeting. The stories of Holocaust survivors show how hatred and intolerance can be sown into an advanced society, turning longtime neighbors and friends into enemies. Hitler and the Nazis created a world where Jews were thought of as a class below animals. Human beings, including members of my family, were seen as vermin to be tortured and ultimately removed from this Earth.

At these events, Holocaust survivors were referred to as an endangered species on their way to extinction. The words stung every time I heard them, insulting me. My ninety-five-year-old grandfather was still alive and I refused to believe he would die anytime soon. The stories of the atrocities of the Holocaust are important, but what may be even more important is what happened after. The survivors are real people, not characters in a movie. Their lives did not end at liberation. Their stories continued.

As I got older, I began to ask Poppy questions about his life experiences, specifically about his story of surviving the Holocaust. It was shocking to realize the superhuman grandfather I idolized my entire childhood had lived through hell. Somehow, the atrocities he experienced did not soil his good heart or selfless character.

There are many lessons to be learned from the way Poppy lived his life following the trauma of the Holocaust. He was a kind and altruistic man who learned to let go of the hate and resentment he once felt for the Nazis. He looked to the limitless potential the future held instead of dwelling on the horrors of the past. Poppy created an incredible life for himself, his children, and his grandchildren full of love, support, and Jewish pride. He taught me healthy relationships with my friends and family were the blueprint for a meaningful life.

Hearing Poppy's story made me reflect on how antisemitism is still present in America. Even though Jews are not being sent to concentration camps or forced to wear stars, they are still ostracized. The antisemitism I experienced made me struggle with my sense of self and my Jewish identity. By watching the way my grandfather reacted to the horrors he experienced, I learned how to become comfortable in my own skin.

This memoir is a love letter to my grandfather and my family. I share the lessons, recipes, and stories from my grandfather that define me. As I compiled my family's stories, I realized the lessons were not limited to those related to me. This book is not a retelling of my life; it is a story of how culture transcends generations through shared family values and cooking. While this story is told through a Jewish lens, it has universal lessons about culture, history, and identity. It is for anyone who wants to connect with their own cultural roots or lineage and understand how that has defined the person they are.

I share some of my favorite memories with Poppy, like cooking Hungarian potato dumplings in his kitchen, as we connect without distractions from the outside world. Time stood still in those moments and everything else seemed to fade away. Through spending time with the people who love us the most, we can learn the best ways to love ourselves and our histories.

CHAPTER ONE

MICHELLE

They say that it takes a village to raise a child. My childhood was no different. I didn't realize for a long time how fortunate I was to grow up with my family. I was unaware if most of my friends' grandparents were alive, let alone who lived nearby all year round. My life was different from my friends in that respect. Their families often fell into the category of snowbirds, flying down south to Boca or somewhere in Florida to avoid the frigid New Jersey winters, but not mine. I can't imagine only seeing my grandparents for major holidays or fleeting visits. Just the idea of spending weeks or months apart makes my heart ache.

My world did not have the capability for such a thing.

I grew up with a huge, loving, *involved* Jewish family. Not only did I have all four grandparents, but two great-grandparents as well. All of whom were deeply ingrained in my day-to-day life. My life was so inextricably linked to that of my grandparents. The pride and joy they got attending every event of mine, from honor society inductions to chorus concerts, and even just stopping by my house, helped me grow into myself. My father's parents, Bubba and Poppa, were my biggest supporters. Bubba was always around for shopping trips, shows on Broadway, or a "girls' chat." Poppa strolled up to every soccer game with a folding chair in one hand and newspaper in the other. He was unmistakable on the sidelines.

My mother's parents, Poppy and Grandma, lived even closer. I saw them constantly. I would go to their house and Grandma would offer me a treat from the beloved candy drawer. Poppy would stop by our house to drop off my favorite snack, blueberries. He stayed for no more than a quick hello before he was on his way. If I wasn't there, the berries would be on the counter waiting for me. When I saw them, I would immediately run to the sink and wash them off. With the phone in one hand and berries in the other, I would thank him between mouthfuls of sweetness. On those rare times I didn't see them, we were always connected and talking on the phone every day. It was always a short conversation ending with Poppy saying, "So take it easy, I speak to you later. I love you," but it was our way of showing we cared and loved each other.

It was a beautiful childhood full of love, support, and, above all else, family.

Jewish tradition and culture surrounded me on both sides. From big family meals on holidays to small Yiddish sayings on a day-to-day basis, my world and sense of self were deeply rooted in my Judaism. Slowly that sense of self was challenged when I was no longer insulated by my family.

Casual antisemitism engulfed my entire life. I can only pick out the few clear-cut and obvious instances because it was part of my everyday life. These microaggressions slowly tore down my self-esteem and increased my anxiety.

Although my town was full of people supposedly like me, most did not understand the fundamental differences between us. My town had a large Jewish population but grandchildren of survivors or recent Jewish immigrants were few and far between. I wasn't far removed from my European roots. I was my happiest smelling sautéed onions on the stovetop or with creamy sour cream resting on my plate. These staples in Jewish and Hungarian cuisine were fragrant with paprika and garlic. When most kids chose Wonder Bread sandwiches, my favorite foods got me off-putting looks in my classrooms. Cottage cheese, especially, was a strange food for a child to eat, let alone the concoction of cottage cheese and noodles with raisins that made my heart soar when I was a small girl.

Sitting at my small table in preschool, I pulled out a brown paper bag with artistically crafted flowers on the front. My mother always drew small sketches on my lunch bags. It was an extra loving touch I looked forward to each and every day as I sat down to eat. Pulling out my small containers to separate the components of my carefully assembled lunch, I saw another girl, Micaela, eyeing me over her peanut butter and jelly sandwich from across the table.

"What *is* that?" she asked with a perplexed and disgusted look on her face.

With my separate containers clearly visible, I shamefully lowered my eyes and combined the noodles, cottage cheese, and raisins for my favorite treat. As I mixed my culinary masterpiece, my stomach grumbled with excitement after a long morning. I was taken by surprise. Liquid started to rise above my noodles, making the raisins float. I looked up to find Micaela pouring her apple juice into my lunch. The splashes of juice dampened my paper bag, making the ink from my mom's flowers start to run. Being around five years old, I cried from nearly everything. Sensitive was an understatement and something I tried to hide under fake laughs and witty comebacks as I grew up.

My teacher later reprimanded Micaela with a call to her parents, but nothing more came of the situation for her. With what, at the time, could only be classified as a traumatizing experience, I vowed to never eat cottage cheese and noodles again. My favorite meal was pushed deep into my memory, ruined for the remainder of my childhood. In that moment, my shame for my cultural heritage only began to grow.

Intolerance increased as I got older. Regardless of the severity and how scary those experiences were, I will never forget the feeling of shame that overcame me when people growing up talked about my Judaism. After the shame came the guilt—the guilt that I should be proud to be a Jew because I knew there was no logical reason I existed in the first place. Somehow my family lived on, but millions of my own people died just for their religion.

The guilt wasn't because anyone told me I should feel guilty for my shame. It was the same guilt I saw reflected in my mother's and aunt's actions. The constant guilt dictated my mom's every decision and led her to put everyone else in front of herself. She didn't complain and she often martyred herself to keep the peace, even in my house growing up. Both she and her sister never felt sorry for themselves. Self-pity was not a luxury they had capacity for. That guilt caused them to put their feelings aside and move forward instead of crying or dwelling.

One day when I was feeling sorry for myself, my mom told me about her childhood dog, Bandito. He was the world's fattest Chihuahua and always picked on by the German shepherds in his prior home. Bandito was instantly drawn to my mom. She thought he was the sweetest and most snuggly dog in the world. Every day when Mom came home from school, Bandito was there excitedly waiting for her. He would run toward her, tail wagging, with a smile across his entire face. His whole body would shake with affection.

As Bandito grew fatter, my mom grew taller. In that time, they became nearly inseparable. In sixth grade, her class spent the year preparing for a trip to Boston. They hosted fundraisers and events to raise money for this class trip as they learned about the history associated with the region. As springtime rolled around, their long-awaited trip finally arrived. The three days in Boston flew by. When she returned home, something was wrong. She was not greeted by a familiar fat and furry face. This time when she came home, there was no Bandito. She started looking around the living room and, in the kitchen, she found Poppy.

"I ran up to him and asked, 'Where's Bandito?' Poppy responded by saying, 'He's dead.' He didn't even flinch." Even sitting on my bed years later, my mom's tone was sharp.

Disbelieving, she ran around the house, looking for his bed, food bowl, or any remnants of him, but it was all gone. As she ran around looking for traces of her puppy, she heard Penny coming up the stairs. My mom flung open the door to the lower level of their split-level house and her eyes welled up with tears as they greeted her sister's.

"When I saw her, she said something along the lines of, 'I don't want to hear it.' I didn't know she was the one who had to take Bandito to the vet when he died."

Penny shut down every emotion except anger. She walked into her room, slamming the door behind her. Without another word, my mom closed her mouth and tried to hold back her tears. Now that the whole house knew, it was the last of the discussion. There wasn't anything else to say or talk about. The dog was dead and gone, so it was time to move on.

"I spent the entire next day crying in school. I needed somewhere I was allowed to cry."

Their household dynamic did not create space for emotional distress. There was no room to discuss feelings and emotions. Poppy, after experiencing much loss earlier in his life, had no sympathy for dwelling. Life was constantly about moving forward. Like many Holocaust survivors, negative emotions were suppressed. Death is part of life, and they all learned death would come eventually for everyone.

For so long I fought to keep the two sides of my identity separate. I wanted anything but to stand out in the crowd for fear of being labeled as different, or, worse, as "too Jewish." Whatever that meant, I felt being connected to my religion and my culture left me ostracized from the secular world. When it all became too much to bear alone, I hid away in my grandparents' small kitchen, cooking every dish from home fries to goulash with spicy Hungarian paprika as the key spice. The separate world we lived in, bonded by peeling potatoes and the smells of spices, was my safe haven, keeping me connected with my roots.

Most of my favorite childhood memories with my grandfather were spent in his kitchen. He was an incredible cook. Notably, every dish was made without a defined recipe. He and I spent hours laboring over meals just to eat them up in a matter of minutes. The time and patience spent creating a meal made it that much more delicious when I was finally allowed to eat.

We would stand huddled over a large bowl, filling it with less-than-scientific measurements to make my favorite comfort food, klutzkahs. These potato dumplings made of flour, eggs, potatoes, salt, pepper, paprika, and seltzer were a staple of my childhood. After making and chilling the dough, we boiled the dumplings and then sautéed them in toasted breadcrumbs and sometimes served them with a little bit of cinnamon and sugar. I could never seem to get the recipe right on my own. The lack of measurements always made it difficult because Poppy would look at the dough and add ingredients until it "felt right."

He started the process by boiling water for the potatoes. Then, he lifted the large heavy pot onto his walker's makeshift tray, which was just a thick piece of plywood and some duct tape, and pushed it over to the side counter. We dumped the potatoes into a colander and then put them into his food mill. Its small handles rested over the bowl, but not well enough to stay on without an extra set of hands. When I was a little girl, he would place his wrinkled hands over mine and we would turn the crank together. Once we were both older, I became his hands. Instead of leading with me as the sous-chef, he instructed from the sidelines. The food mill squeaked as I turned it, grating the potatoes into nothingness.

He directed me in his thick Hungarian accent, "More, more, add more flour. Why are you so stingy with it?" and then proceed to shout, "Ah, that's enough, that's enough. A little too much, but everything is okay." I never had that touch to get them quite right without proper instruction.

Inside his kitchen, time seemed to stand still as we were transported back to Eastern Europe and a different time. We used the simplest appliances and his food mill seemed older than Jewish history itself, reminding us of how another way of life transcended generations. There were no shortcuts or machines to do the heavy work, only our hands and our spirits putting love into the dough and making it just right.

While the sticky dough cooled in the refrigerator to firm up, Poppy and I would walk over to the table. I usually poured some of the remaining seltzer into two small glasses and we would take a sigh of relief as our biceps rested from our ricing and kneading workout.

When we sat at the table, I would probe him with questions about his story of surviving the Holocaust. I longed to know every detail and began to piece together the bits and pieces. When prompted, he answered questions about the life he left behind, but never shared more information than exactly what I requested. Everything he shared about the war was matter of fact and without emotion. It was almost like he was reading out of a history textbook rather than sharing his own experiences and reactions.

For seventy-five years, his story was only in fragments. He took his trauma and put it away on a shelf, vowing to never relive the pain he endured. His years of neutrality allowed him to finally begin to tell his story. As I listened, I tried to empathize with what I imagined he was feeling, but he never expressed his true emotions. When I asked a few too many questions or something a little too emotional, he inevitably responded with his infamous line.

"What is there to say that hasn't been said before? It is what it is. That's part of life."

Then, I would shut my mouth and we would move onto another topic, generally some outrageous things my grandma did that week, like only getting one box of Entenmann's donuts at the store when they were on sale as buy one get one free.

As a kid, I was always confused about the way he acted about the Holocaust. He didn't live bitter and cynical, like in stories I read. He was warm, supportive, and potentially an incredible actor for hiding whatever pain he felt. The good and the bad were all part of life. Anything that happened, he moved forward. Loss was merely another blip on the radar.

Poppy never avoided German products or held strong resentment toward Germany or the German people. He used a Krupps coffeepot every day to make his morning cup. One day, sitting around his kitchen table, I asked him about this. He told me there were two types of survivors: those who moved forward and those who relived the atrocities for the rest of their lives. If survivors were the latter, he explained, then the Nazis won. This unique perspective is why his story, and his life, was unique and deserves to be shared.

CHAPTER TWO

POPPY

———

"I guess we will start at the beginning," Poppy slowly traced small semicircles with his nails on the place mat in front of him as he began to speak. His hands were wrinkled and arched in a half-fist shape from arthritis and years of manual labor. The lines on his hands could be traced like hieroglyphics, telling a story of loss and rebuilding.

"Before the Germans occupied Hungary, conditions were tolerable. It wasn't a picnic, but it wasn't so bad. We had our house and our family. We went about our business as much as possible," Poppy's voice was raspy and deep. His thick Hungarian accent made his Ws sound like Vs. He spoke with a rhythm that accented the end of every sentence. He was a natural orator, compelling me to listen.

"Munkacs was a very Jewish town, you know. It was mixed. We had Czechs, Germans, Hungarians, Russians, and Jews everywhere. Most of the middle-class Jews were Zionist. We had the Gymnasium, where I went to school. It wasn't just the traditional subjects. We also learned Hebrew and Jewish history."

Munkacs was a medium-sized city at the base of the Carpathian Mountains. With the constant border shifts, the town changed countries multiple times over the course of the twentieth century. It was Austria-Hungary, Czechoslovakia, and the Soviet Union at various points in my grandfather's life. He always referred to himself as Hungarian. In turn, so did I.

Although the city changed country affiliations frequently, the character of the town remained constant. In the 1920s and 1930s, there was a thriving Jewish population. Nearly 40 percent of the town was Jewish and it was evident to anyone present. Jews owned the majority of the businesses, so they closed for the weekend. They were closed on Saturdays for Shabbat and closed on Sundays because of Czechoslovakian laws prohibiting business other than food sales. Through the center of Munkacs, there was a large main street full of businesses. The Hebrew Gymnasium became one of the most successful Zionist schools in Eastern Europe. Poppy and his siblings spent countless hours there. Not only were they stuck inside at school all day, but every weekend they went back. The school served as a social event space where they could run around or hang out with their friends.

"Everything in Munkacs depended on the Jews," Poppy lectured me, a constant reminder not to forget the role of Judaism in any city.

The early years of the war hardly affected Munkacs. Life remained nearly the same as before the war. Poppy was only a teenager at the time and the youngest of his siblings. His oldest sister, Bella, was in college in Budapest. Women didn't often go to college, but Bella was an incredible gymnast. With her advanced skills, she received a nontraditional education opportunity. His other older sister, Sidi, and brother, Yoshka, stayed at home in Munkacs to work. As the war grew closer, Poppy was pulled out of high school and became an apprentice with a mechanic. It was meant as a precautionary measure to help give him a trade and value in the war effort. They lived relatively normal Jewish lives.

Friday night began Shabbat, the day of rest. Every week the tradition was the same: starting from when he was a young boy, Poppy's job was to handle the cholent, their Saturday lunch stew. He walked down the road to the baker with a large pot on Friday afternoon. On Saturday morning, after his father returned from praying at synagogue, Poppy walked back and grabbed the silver pot he knew was his. It was heavy and full of rich and hearty stew. The smell of the beans and potatoes was nearly enough to fill his stomach. He slowly carried the pot back, trying to avoid spilling or dropping it.

"Every Friday night, my mom served dinner and fresh challah. She was the most wonderful cook. Saturday lunch was always a big deal." He closed his eyes and my mouth salivated as I imagined the soft dough melting in my mouth. I thought my grandfather was the best cook, but it was clear his mother was on an even higher level.

Usually, family and some of their friends came together to eat. Poppy and his siblings spent Saturdays playing soccer after Shabbat lunch and hanging out at the Zionist Gymnasium with other kids their age.

Poppy's family was not orthodox, nor did he attend synagogue every week, but Saturday lunch was a constant. When they went to shul, they attended the large synagogue in the center of town as opposed to the small shul in their neighborhood. Emerick, Poppy's father, had his own reserved seat in the large shul, which is probably why they chose to go there in the first place. The temple separated men and women with the women high up, looking down from the rafters to see the men below.

Emerick wasn't overly affectionate, but he was a strong patriarch that took care of his family. In many ways, hearing Poppy describe his father's responsibility for the rest of the family reminded me of the way I saw him as the patriarch of ours. Their relationships were built on mutual respect and a sense of providing for the betterment of the entire family, not just the individual.

Their large off-white stone house had plenty of space for all six of them and their housekeeper. Their five bedrooms, living room, and kitchen were lined with photos, art, and Judaica. There was even a garden in the back his mother tended to. It was full of fresh vegetables and succulent fruit trees that bloomed in the summertime. Their neighborhood was very mixed and full of other government employees. They associated with everyone, even people from the nearby German town.

"My father was a well-respected man because he was a big hero in the First World War. We were in a good position. He became a county employee, a tax collector. We had it pretty good. Even when there was a lot of antisemitism, it didn't apply to us. One day, some kids broke a window in our house. The local Gentile kids went and beat them up. They said, you don't touch that house." His face was serious and his brow furrowed slightly. "My family wasn't normal Jews. My father was a Hungarian." He looked at me earnestly, trying to make sure I understood how important that was.

Even in the increasing antisemitism, my grandfather's family was protected. The anti-Jewish laws, like quotas or restrictions in occupations, enacted by the Hungarian government, didn't apply to Emerick or his family. That protection didn't last. In December of 1944, the Germans marched into Hungary and everything changed.

The Germans did not recognize my great-grandfather's past heroism. He was working up until this point, but suddenly lost his job. Yoshka, like many other young Jewish men, was taken to do forced labor and help with the war effort. "The Germans went around saying all Jews must wear yellow stars on their clothing at all times. Every Jew was forced to make the star himself, so my mother did it for me." I sat in the kitchen, imagining my great-grandmother having to mark her son in exile. They lost the status they were accustomed to and were branded. Their entire lives were uprooted.

"Everything moved quickly after the Germans occupied Munkacs. There were no soldiers coming door to door telling people where to move, but we knew what was coming. We heard rumors of what was going on in Poland, that Jews were getting put into ghettos and getting killed. But we heard nothing more than what was on the radio."

In April 1944, almost as soon as the Germans arrived in Munkacs, they forced the Jews to vacate their homes and move into a ghetto in the center of town. The Judenrat, a Jewish Council used to implement and enforce German policies, posted flyers in the streets. These flyers outlined the few items that could be brought in the forced immigration to the center of the city. In less than two days, everyone had to vacate their homes.

"My father yelled at us to hide the seder plate in the attic before we left."

Poppy rushed upstairs to the attic as his father left with handfuls of valuable and sentimental items. Emerick ran over to a house a few doors down.

"Our neighbor promised to hold onto our items until we came back. He was a good friend of the family for a long time. My father trusted him because he was an honest man,"

Poppy's expression softened as he talked in confidence about this man. That promise made by so many neighbors was often not fulfilled.

Without any other options, my grandfather and his family packed a few belongings and said goodbye to their home.

"When we left our home, I didn't know exactly what was going on."

His childlike lightheartedness helped keep him hopeful that things would not be so bad. He continuously reminded himself to remain positive, because the alternative would never benefit him.

In a mass migration, they walked to the center of Munkacs. When they arrived, they were assigned an apartment. The small apartment of a room and a half would have been cramped and uncomfortable for just the four of them after living in such a spacious house. Instead, it was nearly unbearable as they were shoved in with another ten people.

"We were lucky my uncle was in the group that we shared the apartment with. There was no furniture so they could fit more people into the small space. Everyone was forced to sleep on the cold floor and take up as little room as possible."

Together, they tried to create a semblance of normalcy as they used the small stove for meals. Cooking had always brought their family together, but there wasn't much food to go around. The only way to get food was to sneak out of the ghetto into town.

Poppy quickly got a job assisting the elderly and taking carts. Carts were used to carry dead bodies out of the apartments and take them away. I sat there, stunned with how quickly Poppy brushed over the detail, not even stopping to explain what the phrase "taking carts" meant.

Often being around the edges of the ghetto gave him the opportunity to escape. He knew if he could get outside the confines of the walls and hide his yellow star, he could blend in among the townspeople. With his light hair, he could easily pass as a non-Jewish Hungarian. As he performed his daily tasks, Poppy kept a close eye on the Hungarian soldiers controlling the ghetto. They paced back and forth, watching the entrance. When the Zender turned their back, he acted quickly and dashed out. Leaving and not wearing his star were both risks, but it was easy to get out and the supplies he picked up were worth it.

The ghetto was crowded. The Jews from other cities and towns in the Carpathian Mountains were brought into the same small space. The Germans acted quickly and decisively as they continued their march through Hungary. By December of 1944, they reached Budapest and by the end of May, every Jew was either killed or sent to a concentration camp.

The Jews in Munkacs were confined to a few streets with no resources. There was no food or water inside the walls, but still there was a small amount of hope.

"Even before we were sent to the ghetto, we heard the Russian army nearby. There were rumors that the Russians were living in the Carpathian Mountains outside the town."

They thought the Russians were close to coming. Every day, there were whispers of when the Russian army would come and save Munkacs. They could almost taste the freedom the Allied forces would bring. The struggle of life in the ghetto only persisted for a few weeks until early May 1944 when soldiers entered the walls.

"The soldiers told us we had to leave the ghetto. They were liquidating and preparing for relocation." I took in a sharp breath as I listened. When I learned about the Holocaust in school, teachers explained that relocation was a common euphemism for being sent to the concentration camps. I prepared myself for what came next.

That day, the Jews were forced out of their small apartments in the center of the city. Almost as if they were a herd of sheep, they walked to the nearby brick factory. Poppy stayed close to his family, hoping not to lose them in the large crowd. They only walked for a few hours in the middle of the day. Poppy completed the walk with relative ease. He was young and agile, albeit a few weeks undernourished. His usually full stomach hadn't been full in weeks, but he had not experienced real hunger. Not yet.

When they arrived at the brick factory, it was dark. They laid down outside on the earth without blankets to keep them warm or pillows to support their heads. For the next week, they remained in the same spot. One day, Emerick was grabbed by an officer. They kicked him and beat him. He hadn't done anything wrong but being Jewish was reason enough. As Poppy told me about this incident, I felt myself wince, but he remained calm. I searched for feeling in his weathered face, but the only sign of upset came through his words, seemingly lowered in defeat as he recounted the humiliating experience.

The conversations among the Jews were tense and anxious. There was uncertainty about what would happen next. Still, the whispers of Russian liberation continued. The Russians, their only hope for salvation, could have come any time they wanted and saved them, but they never did. Soon, the Jews of Munkacs were loaded onto trains and shipped off to the vast unknown.

Hundreds of people were loaded into cattle cars without food, water, or bathrooms. Standing on top of each other with no room to themselves, no one could sit.

"I couldn't tell if I was at the front, back, or side of the train. All I know is I was pushed against the wall and that kept me up."

It was dark and crowded. He heard children crying, people screaming, and the rancid smell of people urinating on themselves. If they were cattle, they probably would have had better treatment before getting shipped off to their own demise. Poppy didn't know where they were going, but he presumed it would be somewhere inside Hungary. After a day and a half of travel, the train finally stopped. They had reached their destination: Auschwitz.

The train came to a halting stop and the doors quickly opened. It was midday, and the sun was bright on their eyes that had seen little light over the last thirty-six hours. As they arrived, they heard an orchestra. It was faint in the background as the soldiers' demanding shouts overtook their sense of hearing.

"When we arrived at Auschwitz, the soldiers all yelled at us, '*Steigen. Steigen.* Get out. Get out.'"

They quickly poured out of the train and stood, disoriented from the bright light and loud yells of the soldiers. The smoke from the crematoriums filled their nostrils with the smell of burning flesh. They quickly learned how people were killed and their bodies disposed of.

"When we arrived at Auschwitz, people there were saying, 'You smell that? It's your mother. It's your father,'" Poppy said with a heavy sigh. His gaze lowered down to the table, watching his curled fingers continue to trace the half-circle shapes. He took a deep breath before continuing.

Everything happened so quickly, there was no time to think, feel, or process anything. As Poppy explained the remainder of the story, it was in quick succession. He told it one event after the other with no break for reflection or processing emotions. That was the way he told all the events of the Holocaust, as a quick list of events like someone sharing a list of items from the grocery store.

"We stood, lined up, awaiting the selection. Like you hear in the other stories, the elderly and children were separated from the young. Women were in a different line than men. My mother was holding her nephew. Because of this, the Germans assumed she was his mother. Together, they were sent straight to the gas chambers. Sidi was sent to the side with working-aged women and then to Bergen-Belsen."

When I visited Auschwitz in high school, I stood on that same platform my family had nearly seventy years prior. As Poppy spoke, I envisioned my family waiting among the sea of people pouring into Auschwitz. I could picture their faces, serious with their pained eyes full of concern and fear. Sidi, with her soft eyes full of kindness, was sent away to one of the most notorious and painful camps. She was beautiful with soft features. Like many women in the Holocaust, I would not be surprised if she warranted the unwanted attention of Nazi soldiers.

"My father went a different way from me. Later, I found out he was put to work in Auschwitz. He died after a few months working from malnutrition and a cough. I never saw him again."

CHAPTER THREE

POPPY

———

42716. A number and not a name. That day, Poppy was not only stripped of his family but also his identity. That is what the Nazis thought of Jews. They were not seen as individuals with lives or loved ones. Poppy was only seen as another number. By May of 1944, prisoners were processed so quickly that there was no time to tattoo numbers on their arms. After they were assigned numbers, they received itchy striped uniforms and prepared to have their heads shaved.

I sat across from Poppy at his kitchen table, noticing the way the light reflected off the wrinkles on his face. Poppy's bright kitchen did not mirror the heaviness weighing me down. I knew the worst of the story was yet to come.

"The uniform was the same for everyone. It felt kind of like a potato sack. The shoes were whatever they gave you."

They were required to wear the uniform and hat at all times, not that there was any option to change into something more comfortable. Luckily, Poppy received a pair of shoes that somewhat fit. Other prisoners tried to trade to get ones that wouldn't squeeze or fall off their feet.

Poppy was left with his cousins, Mickey and Osce. They sat in the same changing area where another prisoner shaved their heads. Poppy's thick hair fell around him, accentuating his already large ears. He looked over to his cousins. His eyes scanned over their faces, recognizing Mickey's wide nose and Osce's soft features. There was vague resemblance to their past selves. Rather than the kind, lighthearted, and free spirited eighteen-year-old boy who loved to play soccer in the fields, my grandfather became another general prisoner. To anyone not looking closely, each prisoner was unidentifiable from the next.

They were quickly sent off to their barracks to prepare for what came next. As Poppy entered the barrack, he noticed they were lined with wooden bunk beds. He climbed onto the bottom bunk and one prisoner laid on each side of him. Without blankets or pillows, their bodies rested on the plain wooden boards. His group of prisoners waited there for days without food or water.

My chest tightened as I took in a sharp breath. My mouth was dry, unable to imagine the unquenchable thirst Poppy experienced.

Day and night they continued to hear the orchestra. It was the same faint music they heard as the cattle cars pulled up to the camp before the selection. The orchestra was comprised of the most musically talented prisoners. They were forced to play music which was seen as "helpful" to the Germans as part of running the camp. The prisoners were unable to escape the haunting sounds, as the notes reached every corner of Auschwitz in daylight and darkness.

By now it was June, and they could feel the warm summer air. After a few days in Auschwitz, the men separated into Poppy's group were loaded onto trains and taken away once again. The soldiers held guns as they gave orders and barbed wire surrounded them on all sides. There was no option except obeying. Auschwitz was likely a death sentence. They didn't know leaving gave them a greater chance for survival. When the train stopped again, they arrived in the Gross-Rosen work camp Fünfteichen near Braslaw. It was midafternoon and the sun started to lower itself slightly in the sky.

After arriving, the soldiers gave a small speech about their new work assignments and sent them off to the barracks. Fünfteichen was surrounded by electric wire with guard towers every so many yards. There were guards on shift at all hours and prisoners were not allowed to leave their barracks after dark. The few times prisoners were shot were when they left the barracks at night.

"At five a.m., they woke us up to take roll and get counted. We did a few exercises, then we were given *breakfast*," Poppy chuckled as he said the word. As if the meager piece of bread and cheese could even be counted as a meal. It tasted like it was made with sawdust, which wouldn't have been surprising to get more substance out of the dough.

They were woken up to the sound of a gong resonating through the camp. The sky was still dark as the sound carried strongly through the thin wooden walls of the barrack. Poppy rolled out of his shared bed, quickly becoming alert and preparing himself for the harrowing day ahead. The prisoners were lined up outside, shoulder to shoulder, quivering in fear as they prepared for the morning count. Slowly, he began to move, arms reaching up and down. While maintaining a straight face, Poppy did jumping jacks and other exercises under the careful watch of Nazi soldiers to prove his strength for the workday ahead. Each day was a test of if his life was worth living and if he was strong enough to withstand another day of malnutrition and labor.

"Then, we walked thirty minutes to the factory. There were no buildings, no nothing on the way. We just walked until we got to the factory. The supervisors told us what to do and how to do it. I was lucky my father had me study with a mechanic before the war. It gave me a trade that was valuable for forced labor.

Every day was the same. We woke up, we did exercise, we were given what they called food, and then we went to work. Nothing fancy," Poppy described. His tone was flat, and he sounded bored, almost annoyed at having to recount something so monotonous.

Every day they walked the same path back and forth on the way to the factory. It was only a barren landscape. What I failed to ask, and he never mentioned, was what this path looked like. From hearing other Fünfteichen survivor testimonies, I learned it was walked so many times it became almost a dirt road they followed between two narrow layers of barbed wire, preventing them from moving sideways in either direction. On the outside of the barbed wire, soldiers barked orders and dogs bit at them if they got too close (Holocaust Matters, 2022). Any details about his experience needed to be carefully extracted like in a game of Operation, otherwise he started to get impatient with me and went off on tangents that made it clear our conversation was done for the day.

They arrived at the Krupps Munitions Factory, where Poppy did mechanical work on parts for tanks. It was a military factory supplying parts for the war effort. Day in and day out he worked on the same machine. He was in a huge room with other men, and they spoke minimally as they worked. The supervisors in the factory observed their work. Prisoners were punished if they didn't work, talked too much, or did a bad job. Poppy avoided punishment by keeping his head down and doing what he was told. His joking attitude remained repressed under his serious demeanor, but he still spoke here and there to the men standing next to him. They were just thankful their rules weren't as serious as the other work camps they had heard about.

"When we were done with work, we walked back. They gave us what they called soup. It was mostly warm water with a little piece of meat or a vegetable. Then, we went back to the barracks. We couldn't leave when it was dark out to use the bathroom or nothing or we'd get shot."

As they arrived at their barracks, they laid on the plain wooden boards, trying to sleep before repeating the whole day over again. They worked day after day in this monotonous routine, just doing as they were told and trying to avoid punishment from any soldiers in particularly bad moods. There were no selections specifically, but sometimes if workers were not in good shape, they were shot or transported out and never returned.

One night, the man in charge of Poppy's barrack was ripped from his bed. He was a Jew from Holland, but apparently not very good at his job. Outside of the barrack, they punched and beat him. The prisoners in the barrack remained quiet and still. They heard every sound of the beating, the sobs and screams of the prisoner and the crunching of his bones.

"When the man stopped screaming, we knew that was it. He was beaten to death. That night, no one said anything," Poppy looked off in the distance as he shared. I couldn't understand how he kept his neutrality as he told the brutal story. Without a moment of hesitation, he resumed.

The German winter was bitter and cold. All of the prisoners were weak and their stomachs hurt from malnutrition. Their once strong youthful muscles had atrophied. They were skeletons of what people are supposed to be. Their meager daily portions were not enough to sustain them. No one could even steal extra food because there was none. The war effort became so weak that there weren't enough supplies to go around. One extra cold night, the Germans needed prisoners to shovel coal and heat the camp.

They called out Poppy's number and, in the middle of winter, he set out to perform his work. He shoveled the heavy coal and the labor did little to warm his freezing body. The uniform did next to nothing in keeping him warm or protecting him from hypothermia. The malnutrition combined with freezing temperatures caused Poppy to get sick and he was sent to the infirmary.

In the infirmary, he recognized the doctor from his home in Munkacs. I could only imagine Poppy's relief of seeing someone he trusted. This infirmary would be a safe place for him to recover.

"Every day, the doctor came and checked on me. He couldn't do much. The Germans were losing the war, so there was no extra food he could bring me."

The doctor did his best to keep Poppy comfortable. He stayed there for a few weeks and was discharged two days before liberation.

"He came up to me one day and told me he heard they were evacuating the camp soon," Poppy softened his facial expression, lifting his eyes to meet mine as he spoke. "He told me, 'I tried to keep you here as long as I could.' I think he was signing that I was still sick because the sick were usually left behind."

When the doctor couldn't keep Poppy there any longer, Poppy and Mickey decided their best option was to stay at the camp. The German transport began to leave, taking the prisoners with them. Mickey and Poppy managed to hide underneath the beds within the small infirmary of the camp. After spending the past few weeks there, he knew the infirmary like the back of his hand. Mickey and Poppy knew leaving with the Germans would put them on a death march. Osce decided to take his chances on the march and left, and was never seen by his brother or cousin again.

CHAPTER FOUR

POPPY

——

As the transport disappeared into the distance, there should have been silence. Instead, the commanding sound of two SS officers' footsteps was overpowering. Poppy and Mickey couldn't tell if the footsteps were strong enough that the whole building was shaking, or it was just their bodies. Their hearts pounded so loudly they worried the soldiers could hear it from the entrance. As the soldiers entered the infirmary, Poppy and Mickey were certain the officers had come to kill anyone who hid. Hidden underneath the beds, they looked at each other, paralyzed in fear, and prayed they had enough luck to survive. The soldiers entered through the door, standing tall and serious with rifles in their hands. They took a quick scan of the room from the entryway and, without saying a word, turned around and walked away.

"If those soldiers had taken a closer look, they would have easily found us. After those soldiers left, we still didn't go anywhere. In the infirmary, there was nothing. We had no food, no water, and no bathroom."

They remained hidden for only four days, but it felt like weeks. There were no clocks to give them a sense of how long it was since the march left. They stayed there in silence, afraid to move or leave the infirmary in case some soldiers had stayed beyond to shoot anyone that hid. Their adrenaline, fear, and hope overpowered the hunger and dehydration. At least there was some amount of safety in being hidden. The whispers leading up to the evacuation, that the Russians were closing in, finally came true. They heard air raids over the previous few weeks which added to the reliability of the rumors. Their anticipation was high. Finally, the rumors were confirmed true as Russian soldiers entered the camp.

Liberation had finally come.

The energy in Poppy's house lifted and the sun started to shine brighter, illuminating the photo on the wall behind him and the entire kitchen. The lump in my throat disappeared as I listened to the beginning of the hopeful part of his journey.

In a whirlwind, their entire lives changed. The six prisoners hidden in the infirmary were free men. Their first thought was basic bodily needs. The group rushed straight to the kitchen, hoping to find some amount of nourishment, but the kitchen was barren and empty.

Regardless, it was a new day. They were so happy just to be alive. Their smiles extended from ear to ear in a grin that they were no longer just numbers used for forced labor. The sobering reality of their situation hit them. Mickey and Poppy looked at each other with somber smiles on their faces. They had survived, but they wondered how many others were so lucky. There was only one way to find out. Their eyes met as they nodded their heads in agreement.

"Let's go home," they said.

With a smile at sharing the same thought aloud, Poppy put his arm around his cousin. Together, Poppy and Mickey walked out of the barbed wire gates of the camp.

They went into an abandoned town nearby they had not seen when walking to the factory each day over the last seven months. The whole surrounding town was empty, without a German soldier or civilian in sight. They walked into the evacuated German homes, noticing the soldiers had left so abruptly that there was still food left on their tables. Every civilian nearby had left with the army. It was late, so they chose a house to rest and slept on their first real beds in almost a year.

The beds embraced them like a warm hug as their tired bodies collapsed into the mattresses. Pillows held up their heads and blankets kept them warm from the frigid winter air. Finally, they were able to rest and were in awe of the safety a comfortable bed could provide.

The next morning, they packed as much as they could from the abandoned house, preparing for the long journey ahead. They didn't know how long it would take to get home, so they packed everything they could find. They changed out of their prisoner uniforms into civilian clothes from the house. They were skinny and weak. As he looked in the mirror, Poppy noticed his hair had turned from golden blonde to prematurely white from stress and malnutrition. His once defined muscles had atrophied, and his skin hugged the bones where muscle used to be. They began their long trek back home in what they assumed was the right direction but were soon stopped by a Russian soldier.

"The Russian soldier asked us where we were going. We said we were going home to Munkacs and were liberated from forced labor camp. He laughed and told us we were going the wrong way! He told us the Germans were over the way we were going."

Poppy and Mickey couldn't help but laugh as they turned around and went on their way. They were walking west to

Germany as opposed to east back to Munkacs. As they walked, the weight of food, clothing, and supplies they packed were too heavy to bear. They unloaded more and more weight as they traveled. By night, there was nothing left. They stopped in an abandoned German home to spend the night. This pattern held for a few days, walking then resting in an abandoned home before moving on.

As they walked, they saw the outline of a large bridge. The sharp January wind ripped through their thin clothing, and they shuddered thinking about how cold the water must be below. The river was wide and deep, rushing quickly by. As they walked closer, they recognized it as a military bridge. There was no walking area, and it was off limits to civilians. They stopped to contemplate their next steps when they saw a Russian soldier in the distance standing near his car.

As they approached him, they could smell the alcohol on his breath. He was standing up straight enough that they weren't convinced of his inebriated state. Without any other options, they asked, "Can you give us a ride across the way? We can't get across on foot."

The soldier agreed as he finished his drink and they all climbed into the car. The car moved slowly, riding up the bridge. As they continued, the car began to veer. As if in slow motion, the car drove off the side of the bridge. Before they knew what happened, they were barreling down into the freezing water.

The car's doors weren't securely shut, so Poppy pushed the door out. Mickey did the same and they began to move. Their weak arms plowed forward through the water, trying not to let the cold overtake them. Using whatever energy they had gained over the previous few days, they swam. Stroke after stroke, they cut across the icy water. It could have been luck, or forces beyond their control, but their hands reached dry land. They had not just survived a war to be taken out by some cold water.

One after the other, they hoisted themselves up onto dry land. Lying down on the frosted grass, they took a few moments to catch their breaths.

When Poppy told me this story, seated around his kitchen table, I asked him about what happened to the Russian officer.

With a gentle laugh, he casually responded, "He was fine. Well, I think he was probably fine. He wasn't *that* drunk and could probably swim. After the bridge, we walked to Poland."

As they arrived in Poland, they knew papers were necessary to continue their voyage.

They saw a church in the center of town and decided that would be the best place to start. The priest was kind and welcoming, allowing them to stop and relax for a while. In this time, he was able to acquire papers for them from the local police.

"The Polish were very religious people, you see, so that's how we chose to go to the church. You know, this guy was the Pope!" Poppy noted before continuing his story.

Upon their arrival at the church, the priest asked if they had eaten breakfast and they replied that they had not. As they were welcomed into the church, they were greeted by the aromatic saltiness of freshly cooked bacon.

The eating area had a long table with a feast laid out across it. Poppy's mouth salivated thinking about having a warm and filling meal. The table was covered with plates of eggs, fresh rye bread, and bacon. It was nothing like the breakfasts he grew up with, but he couldn't take his eyes off the sight of crispy, caramelized bacon before him. He had never eaten pork before.

Jews and bacon. Generally, an unsightly pairing, especially in my kosher household. In middle school, I became a vegetarian and was never too fond of meat to begin with. The sight and smell of pork nauseated me more than anything else. I would see the grease lining the pan in a hotel fresh-to-order kitchen and my stomach would quickly begin to turn. Bacon would just never be for me.

For Poppy, on the other hand, bacon was the greatest food in the world. His mouth watered as bacon hit the only non-kosher frying pan in his house. As the bacon began to sizzle and crack, Poppy always thought of the point in his journey home where he and Mickey found refuge in that Polish church. As he told me the story, his eyes lit up.

He turned to look over at Mickey for approval, who shrugged and filled his own plate. Mickey was never much for following the rules, and who was Poppy to deny a hot meal? They could probably spin the situation to say they were keeping in the spirit of Pikuach Nefesh, watching over the soul, which puts preserving life over following Jewish laws. In reality, they were starving and tired. Keeping kashrut was the last thing on their minds. They piled their plates and felt the greasy crispness warm their bodies from head to toe. This was the feeling lost in the camps throughout the war: freedom.

It took me a long time to understand my traditional Jewish grandfather's love for bacon. To him, bacon wasn't just a food. It was a feeling of freedom that allowed him to open the next chapter of his life. Moving forward, he had to come to a crossroads between the identity he once had and the new life in front of him.

After three weeks of walking and hitchhiking, Poppy and Mickey finally saw the Carpathian Mountains in the distance. Their grandness and beauty were breathtaking. Their eyes watered as they took in the backdrop of their childhood. I could only imagine what it was like to finally return home after being forcibly removed and sent through hell. The mountains symbolized the unlimited potential for their lives, and the hope that still lived on in their hearts.

When he left in the spring, the mountains were lush green with grassy fields sprawling out in every direction. Now, their snowcapped peaks almost faded into the foggy clouds and the colorful sky as the sun set to the west. The white snow cascaded down their sides and Poppy was transported back to memories of his childhood, spent skiing down them.

Full of hope and anticipation, but also fear for what they would find, the two cousins finished the last leg of their long voyage home. When they arrived in Munkacs, very few Jews were there. It was late. The sky was nearly black, and the faint light of the moon guided them. They decided to cross through a field on their way as a shortcut. Little did they know of their transgression.

"We were walking and heard a loud voice. A Russian soldier asked us what we were doing out so late. We froze, we didn't know what to do. So, we told him we were going home from forced labor camp." This was a far too common saying he repeated over the last three weeks.

As the Russian explained the curfew, Poppy fidgeted in his steps. His eyes darted, knowing no one else was outside with them. His mind raced, trying to find an escape route if the soldier didn't let them off easy. He started to speak, outlining the journey he just went through only to be stopped a few kilometers from home.

Their interrogation halted. The soldier's tired eyes gave away that he didn't want to enforce the extreme orders. Finally, he let them go. Their pulses returned to the normal pace and color rushed to their faces. Mickey and Poppy walked down the paved street of Bielekova Boulevard to find Poppy's childhood home.

"When we got there, it was almost the same. From the outside, there were only a few broken windows." It was shocking that through all the looting, bombs, and destruction, his off-white stone house with the slanted grey roof remained virtually unchanged. It was poetic that it was preserved, almost waiting to welcome him back in.

They walked through the house, feeling the profound emptiness. Its large backyard was full of overgrown fruits and vegetables normally harvested in the summertime. The walls were barren with the faint outline of where pictures used to be. All the furniture that had filled the space, making it cozy and warm, was gone. The emptiness was deafening and encompassing because it was more than possessions the Germans took. There were no beds, no blankets, or pillows. That night, they rested on the floor of the place Poppy used to call home, hoping for a better tomorrow.

The next day, someone in town let him know who had taken his family's furniture and possessions. His naivete and desperation led him to walk up and knock on the door of that house. A man came to the front door and Poppy asked kindly if he could have his furniture back. After a minute, the man returned to the door, shotgun in hand.

"He said, 'You want your furniture? Here's your furniture. Get out of here, you dirty Jew.' He laughed and was ready to shoot us." My body was paralyzed as Poppy breezed through this story. It was unimaginable that he was put in so many life-or-death situations one after the other.

Doing the only thing he could, Poppy turned around and walked away. He knew there was no point in ever returning to acquire his stolen possessions. He walked back to his home and knocked on the door of his neighbor who they had given china and other valuables to hide. Unlike the thief from earlier in the day, the neighbor smiled as he returned what he was tasked with holding onto.

Honesty, one of Poppy's highest values, was not gone. Not all the people left in Munkacs took advantage of the situation. As Poppy described the neighbor, his reverence for the man was apparent.

A few days later, Poppy returned to his house. He went up to the attic and collected all the possessions he could find stored there. The pictures, plates, and jewelry hidden were still there. He dug through the basement to find gold and valuable possessions buried, filling two big suitcases. One item stuck out among everything he found: his family seder plate, reminding him of his family. He had no idea if he would ever have those same feelings of family and connectedness again.

CHAPTER FIVE

POPPY

———

The seder plate's off-white color was coated in dust, but its intricate details looked exactly the same. The plate was beautiful and simple with a Jewish star in the middle and six dips, one for each item on the seder plate. It had gold Hebrew letters and was textured outside the dips with little pebbles. As he held the plate, Poppy traced his fingers over each of the grooves. His fingers followed the lines and lightly touched each letter. Somehow, he couldn't find any chips or cracks. The plate reminded him of a simpler time, before the loss and tragedy of the war.

"Before Passover started, we cleaned the entire house. We cleaned room by room to prepare for the big seder we held. The first room we had to clean a few weeks before. We had to store everything there. I remember, we ordered matzah bundled in five kilo packages from a special kosher bakery. The last room to get cleaned was the kitchen. My mom would wake up very early and clean the kitchen. It was so clean you could lick the floors." Poppy's voice was dreamlike.

His mom always began preparations for the seder in the early morning. She cooked a huge dinner of all different Jewish foods, including chicken soup, chicken, red meat, lots of latkes, and she even made her own gefilte fish. While not uncommon at the time, it was still an ambitious task to take on. The seder was always a big meal with about fifteen or twenty people each day, piling into the house. They had cousins and family over, sometimes even inviting friends who needed a place to go. That's what a seder was all about. They would have shiva brucha, who were kids who came up from the small cities and farms to study with the rabbi. Everyone who needed a place to go had a seat at their table. His father's family did not live nearby, so they usually didn't come for any of the holidays.

The seder began after daybreak and went sometimes until midnight or one o'clock in the morning. Just like my family stops after the festive meal, his family never did the entire seder from beginning to end. It was a big party with everyone talking and eating the entire time. The youngest always recited the four questions, and sometimes Poppy was stuck with the task, but not always. The four questions explain why the Passover seder is different than all other nights. They outline the traditional customs of Passover, like why participants must eat matzah, bitter herbs, dipping food, and recline in chairs.

In Poppy's family back then and in my family now, everyone joked as they talked about the wise, the wicked, the simple, and the childhood who did not know enough to ask. They were full of jest as they assigned who at the table was each child.

Halfway through reading the story of Passover from the Haggadah, the children would sneak away from the table, off to hunt for the prestigious afikomen. The hiding of the afikomen is a custom where a piece of the middle matzah is hidden and searched for by children. This piece of matzah is supposed to be the last thing eaten at the seder. It is used to keep children engaged as the long and arduous meal continues for hours on end.

Poppy wasn't too good at finding it. Usually, his parents let relatives and friends' kids look for it since they were guests. It was a tradition to let them look and it was nicer for them to find it and receive their prize. The prize so sought after was a little bit of money, depending on who found it and how his father felt that day. Sometimes Poppy's parents felt bad if some children didn't get it so they would get the reward too. It was mostly a fun thing to bring high spirits into the house. After the meal ended, everyone sat down to talk for about ten minutes instead of continuing the rest of the seder.

The family would also come over for other holidays and spend time together, but nothing ever compared to Passover. They would come for all the holidays like Sukkot and Simchat Torah, which was his favorite. After they finished praying, they went from one house to another for kiddish. By the end, they went to most of the houses. After drinking and eating at each stop, some people were already falling over themselves because they were drunk.

"That plate I found came with me to America. We used it in our house when your mother was growing up and now at Penny's every year," Poppy beamed, knowing our family history was preserved through a single item.

Holidays at my Aunt Penny's house are like when the circus comes into town. It comes in with a whirlwind of people, food, and sounds. People come from far and wide but, before you know it, everyone vanishes. Those were my favorite times of year. Rosh Hashanah, Passover, Thanksgiving, or any other excuse is used to get forty-plus people in her castle of a home.

Penny has always loved to entertain and be the ringleader. Even growing up, she called the shots. She is six years older than my mother, but many confuse them for each other now since they have high cheekbones, similarly shaped faces, and identical mannerisms. My grandparents worked countless hours in my mother's childhood, so for most things they deferred to Penny. Maybe it is the five-inch Jimmy Choo heels she can never be seen without, but her confidence and intelligence radiates, giving her an authoritative presence.

My favorite tradition was that dinner started the minute I walked in the garage door. The front door was too formal an entrance for close friends and relatives. My immediate family was always among the first people to arrive, but food was already lining the counters and tables. We started eating, drinking, and conversing before we could get two steps into the house.

From the second I opened the door, there was a symphony of smells perfectly playing together. As I walked closer to the center of the house, the kitchen, there were two frying areas for latkes. One was gluten-free and ran by Bella's daughter, Linda, and the other was ran by Penny. Poppy was always seated at the countertop across from Penny's, grabbing potato pancakes quickly onto his plate. He gave me his instead of having to fight to snatch a latke as it came off the griddle. We loaded our potato pancakes with applesauce to try to cool them before they burned our mouths. They're best when they're straight out of the fryer, so there's no point in waiting until they get soggy and cold at dinner.

Everyone in my family has their place on the assembly line. Working like a well-oiled machine, we prepare dishes for the masses. My cousin Danny and I have been on potato-peeling duty since we were old enough to hold a peeler. Hunched over the garbage, we peeled enough pota-toes to seemingly support the entire country of Ireland itself. Depending on the occasion, there were as many as twenty dishes in the main course, ranging from my grandmother's traditional luchen (noodle) kugel to a butcher's shop of meat and plenty of vegetables to stuff my vegetarian stomach to the brim. Passover's menu differed slightly, but the only way an outsider would know of the dietary restrictions would be seeing the sheets of matzah on the table. Matzah, the unleavened bread reminding me of a stale cracker, is the universal sign of Passover. It represents the bread that didn't have time to rise and cooked on the Israelites backs as they left Egypt.

I can remember back to the last seder we all shared together before I went off to college. It will be deeply ingrained in my mind as the perfect family meal and the epitome of family holidays growing up. My aunt's house had a large kitchen in the center. The cabinets were a deep mahogany and played off the light granite countertops. The island separated the living room from the kitchen and acted as a serving station for our buffet-style dinner. The living room appeared even grander with its beautiful, vaulted ceilings. They reached nearly twenty feet high and opened the space crowded by a mob of people.

As we sat down around a large square constructed out of tables, I looked down to the Maxwell House Haggadah. It was barely thicker than a Broadway playbill. With my half-full stomach, I prepared for at least two hours of reading ahead. Sitting in the center of the table as the star was Poppy's seder plate. Uncle Brad, Penny's husband, would lead the seder and, being a politician, he never forgot to add his own commentary, making the reading even longer.

I was still the baby of the family and forced to read the four questions. Even though I said the same prayer for over twenty years, my heart always raced with anticipation for the few pages leading up. As a child, I had a Passover cassette tape that played in my car all year round. My mom loathed listening to that tape on repeat but was comforted slightly by my love for something with a consistent connection to Judaism. The Passover songs were so ingrained in my memory, but I always feared forgetting the words when the moment really counted. I softly recited the questions, hoping my complete lack of singing ability would be difficult to notice.

"*Ma Nishtanah Halailah Hazeh Mikol Haleilot.*" *Why is this night different from all other nights?*

This night was different because I was surrounded by my family on all sides. Being in this house was an alternate universe to the world I lived in outside. Everyone knew me for exactly who I was, and I didn't have to hide parts of myself around them. There was no one to impress and it was nearly impossible to offend anyone. This feeling was missing in all other aspects of my life: a sense of self, community, and belonging.

I finished my solo and the show went on. Fortunately, one of the four glasses of wine did not come long after the four questions, so I quickly calmed my heart pounding loudly in my chest. My mom's cousin Donna, always equipped with a sarcastic joke, poured my glass to the brim. Seders traditionally include four glasses of wine throughout, praying and drinking at different points. Everyone able to read traded off reading paragraphs one after the other. We all joined together as parts of one collective unit, trying to keep the flow moving at a comfortable pace. We drank, read, and sang, most of us off-key, for what seemed like eternity before the best part and the main event: the festive meal.

As soon as the reading stopped, me, my mom, Penny, and her kids ran to the kitchen to start dinner service. As graceful as a seasoned waiter who was a few drinks in, we took soup and appetizer orders consisting of "melon, liver, or fish," carefully selecting priority in who got the first plates. Usually, it was reserved for the oldest members, like Poppy, then guests before serving everyone else. Jewish hospitality is like that. Our custom ensures we respect our elders first and foremost. Then we move on to new people, making them feel welcomed and like they belong at our table. Over the years, we hosted a wonderful array of people at our festive meals. My Uncle Brad even once got our local congresswoman to attend the Passover seder.

Even after the meal ended, dinner duty was not over. We swiftly picked up the plates, washing and drying then putting them away at a speed that would make The Flash stop in his tracks. We knew each other's movements so well from the years of practice that it was a mindless activity to set up and break down a meal that fed a small army.

The energy in the house was always electric. Even thinking about it now, I can feel the love and warmth of our wide family tree. Both sides of Penny's and Brad's family came together, making us one single unit. Definition of "cousin" or "family" didn't matter. Holidays at Penny's embraced the Jewish concept of taking in anyone who doesn't have a place to celebrate, just like Poppy's did in Munkacs. People came from far and wide for our Passover seder. My house growing up was only two miles away, but if someone named a place in the tri-state area, my family came from it.

Sitting in his attic, holding his family's seder plate, Poppy had no idea the importance of what was in his hands. That seder plate would tie together generations through Jewish tradition.

CHAPTER SIX

POPPY

——

As he held the plate, his heart sank into his stomach. Each smooth edge was another reminder that his family was broken. Even if the plate had survived the war unscathed, many of his family members had not.

"What can I say about Bella? She was always a beautiful girl. Even when I was a kid people would say how beautiful she was." As Poppy spoke, I saw the sides of his mouth curl upward. He closed his eyes as he pictured his sister. Warmth and affection radiated from Poppy as he reminisced about his sister.

After he and Mickey waited in Munkacs for a few weeks, people slowly trickled back. Desperate for his family to reunite, the day finally came. Bella, his beautiful sister, returned to him. Her radiant youthfulness shined duller than it had before the war. She was very skinny, nearly emaciated, from the months of starvation. Although the war had changed them all, she was still the dynamic soul she had always been.

Bella was the star of her own movie. The world revolved around her, and even if it didn't, Poppy would not be the one to tell her. That was their relationship. They protected one another and it was a promise they kept for the rest of their lives.

Even though she passed when I was nine years old, Bella is a character deeply ingrained in my memory. She had the kind of presence that all eyes would turn to look the moment she walked into the room. She was always dressed to the nines in whatever the fashion was at the time. Her commanding energy caused even her clothing to listen to her. Pantyhose wouldn't dare run on her. She was beautiful and put together. Her strength was unparalleled and her ability to regulate her emotions made everyone see her life as the perfect one she envisioned, even when it wasn't.

"It wasn't some big event when she came back," Poppy stated in his typical bluntness. "We didn't cry. We hugged and we were happy to be reunited. What else is there to say?"

Poppy wasn't sentimental in describing their reunion, but there was an innate comfort once they were back together. They were safe. It was almost like taking in air without realizing you had previously been holding your breath.

"Seeing her after not knowing what happened was mostly just relief."

They remained in Munkacs for a few weeks, collecting their items and seeing which other friends and family would return.

Bella knew their sister, Sidi, had already made it to Budapest.

Sidonia, Sidi for short, was the third child. Unlike Bella, she was more soft-spoken. They were almost opposite in nature, with Bella being outgoing and Sidi doing anything she could to not draw much attention to herself. Sidi was equally as beautiful as Bella but understated. The warm, comforting energy around her and her perpetual smile had somehow not disappeared despite the horrors she experienced.

"Sidi and her boyfriend, Imre, were together as long as I can remember. They were inseparable."

Like most other Jews, during the war, Sidi was ripped away from the people she loved. After surviving Bergen-Belsen, she had no idea if any family members, or Imre, survived. There was only one option now the war was over: travel to Budapest. After the war ended, the Hungarian Jews traveled to Budapest to register at the Great Synagogue, hoping to find the names of loved ones who survived. As Sidi walked out of the Great Synagogue, she spotted a familiar figure among the masses of people and sea of faces. She locked eyes with the figure. There he was, Imre, standing across the street from her. Through all the tragedy and loss, it was b'sheret, fate, that their love persisted.

After a little less than a month, Poppy and Bella decided the only thing to do now was to move forward. Bella and their cousin Iszo had a friend affiliated with the Russian army. They arranged for him to transport two suitcases of some of their family possessions to Budapest. They gave him some of the little money they had, and he left, never to be seen again.

"Everything the Gentiles had saved for us, a Jew just took away," Poppy's hands curled tighter as he spoke. The warmth from talking about his sister quickly dissipated, leaving only cutting words. With disappointment written across his face, his eyes lowered to avoid my gaze as he spoke.

Bella and Poppy said goodbye to Munkacs and their home as they began their trip to join Sidi in Budapest. They both knew, deep down, they would never come back. This was no longer the haven they grew up in. Everything had changed. They would never be the same people they were when they lived at Eleven Bielekova Boulevard. This goodbye was closing the book on the life they once knew. It was permanent. While the journey home was long and difficult, there was still a much longer way to go until he was there with my family around Penny's table.

CHAPTER SEVEN

MICHELLE

—

My hideouts of holidays at my aunt's house and cooking in Poppy's kitchen closed at the end of the weekend. As the school week started, I was shoved back into my complicated reality. Middle school was not an easy time for anyone, with hormones running wild and everyone doing their best to be cool and fit in. It was even harder because I stuck out like a sore thumb. My Jewish star necklace seemed to be a neon sign signifying my "otherness."

On a warm spring day, I walked down the halls of Hammarskjold Middle School. The white walls and large windows of the brand-new building made every cavern of the school full of light. It was bright and evident we were the first grade breaking in the finished product of an eight-year construction project.

As I was about to turn the corner into the lunchroom, something was thrown in front of my feet. I heard the subtle clinging of a small object hitting the ground. The shiny copper penny stopped rattling and sat there, looking up at me. I looked over to see a small group of boys laughing and knocking each other on the arm in jest.

"Jews like pennies, don't they?" The boys cackled wickedly.

I rolled my eyes and crushed the penny beneath my foot as I kept walking, attempting to not engage. I knew there would be no good outcome from retorting back. The other students around me continued about their business. The girl I walked with didn't hesitate in her stride as she raced down the hallway. Everyone else thought it was completely harmless but I couldn't stop thinking back to the sound of that penny hitting the ground. A few class periods after, my Jewish peer told our class of his latest triumph.

"They just threw some change in front of me and started laughing. So, you know what I did?" He laughed in the cocky demeanor of someone who knew they were the smartest person in the room. "I told them, if you're gonna throw money at me, at least make it dollars."

Hearing his response made me fidget in my seat. There was nothing funny about engaging with the stereotypes that had negatively affected our people for centuries. At thirteen, these jokes and stereotypes weren't serious, but these views had turned into reasons for scapegoating and persecution time and time again in Jewish history. Every antisemitic comment or joke felt deeply personal. That night, I returned home and locked myself in my bedroom to be tormented by my own thoughts.

They all think Jews are cheap and like money. They are responsible for every bad thing that has ever happened in the world. Some people even think the Holocaust was justified. What if there is no place for us here?

My heart started to pound. It was the only thing drowning out the intrusive thoughts and repetitive loud clinging of the penny on the tile floor. I sobbed uncontrollably as the pounding filled my ears. My chest tightened and my mind went blank as I clutched my knees in toward my chest, trying to let the tears and screams be an outlet for the pain I couldn't expel quickly enough from my body.

Nights like that became more commonplace, but I attributed it to teenage drama. Every few years they would be accompanied by a recurring nightmare. These outbursts of undiagnosed panic would only progress as I continued my path for perfection, overachievement, and unrelenting desire for reaching unrealistic standards. As my tears died down, my mind came back to the triggering cause of my discomfort: the antisemitism I experienced and my classmate's reaction to it. It was possible I was being a brooding teenager, but more likely I felt my family's trauma couldn't be understood by people who hadn't experienced it.

Only two years earlier I visited the most famous tribute to the Holocaust. Yad Vashem sat atop a hill outside of Jerusalem and taught thousands of people about the atrocities of the Holocaust. Walking into the museum, I felt the hot dry air of an Israeli summer sticking my T-shirt to my back. Beads of sweat dripped down my temples but the arid breeze evaporated them in a moment. Poppy stood next to me, anxiously waiting to enter. His discomfort was apparent as his lips pursed together. He shuffled back and forth as we stood in line. Waiting at the entrance, a tall figure approached my family. He was slender and young with a green uniform and tanned olive skin.

"How old are you, Miss?" the soldier asked.

"I'm ten years old," I responded, confused.

He stepped aside and I continued toward the glass doors as my mother whispered gently in my ear, "I guess you just made the age cut."

Even though I was only ten, I knew the Holocaust all too well. The heartbreak and loss of the Jewish people wasn't just history to me. I saw it on a daily basis as I looked at my grandfather's tired eyes. We stepped into the museum as a rush of cool air conditioning hit us. I gazed up, finding the triangular prism shape of the museum strange. As I looked down the long corridor, I saw ropes and paths weaving back and forth, preventing any viewer from skipping to the end. As we began to walk, a video played and my family stopped. My grandfather grabbed my hand and we saw children singing Hatikvah softly and beautifully. At the bottom of the screen read the words *Munkacs, Hungary.*

"Poppy, isn't that where you are from?" I questioned.

"Yes, it is," he responded softly. "The children singing are from my school. I may be one of them."

As the song slowly faded out, we walked along the path following our guide. I could not stop thinking about what Poppy said about that being his school and his hometown. I looked over at him. He was looking quickly at the exhibits before moving onto the next. He moved ahead of my mother and me as we fixated on the posters of propaganda from the rise of Hitler and Nazi Germany. He moved much faster than us, taking a quick glance and then moving on. My mom and I stopped at every caption, reading, and soaked in the rich history it shared.

As we looked from exhibit to exhibit, I clutched my mother's hand. I gave her a tight squeeze to let her know how much I needed her ever-present strength to hold me up. Her arm reached out and over me, pulling me in close.

"You're okay. I know this is hard," she whispered in my ear before giving me a kiss on my forehead.

Her touch always made me feel stronger and more capable of taking on the world and its challenges. Where others saw our bond as uncharacteristically close of a parent and child, I saw it as a sign of mutual assurance. It was the same way with my grandfather. Having him by our sides, even without words of affirmation supporting us, let us know we would be okay.

Whenever my mom saw pictures from the Holocaust, she looked for her family. She scanned the photos for Poppy, Bella, or her grandparents. Without even really knowing what they looked like at the time, she still searched. She probably wouldn't have recognized them, but it didn't matter. She looked anyway and then so did I.

As she went through the photos, she shared with me her recurring dream. "Starting from when I was a little girl, I had this dream. Somehow, we found Yoshka, Poppy's brother. It was like a soap opera where someone got shot, but they didn't really die. The rest of the characters just thought they did. By some magical turn of events, I discovered he survived and had a new life with a new family. By a twist of fate, he, Poppy, Bella, and Sidi would all be reunited again," as my mom spoke, there was lightness in her voice. She knew it wasn't realistic, but that feeling never left her. Miracles were still possible.

As we walked through the halls of Yad Vashem, my face was wet with tears. Every person whose story I heard resonated deeper than the last. I kept looking for Poppy, wanting to hold or be held by him. I wanted to be reassured that we were okay; we were still here when so many others were not.

As we left and boarded the bus, the guide handed out sandwiches for lunch. My face was stiff from the dry tears and my mother held my hand as I tried to stop myself from sobbing again. My stomach was still in my throat and only hurt more as I tried to hold in the tears. My mom put the sandwich away in her bag, storing it for safekeeping and waiting for my appetite to return.

These feelings shifted when I reached high school. They transitioned from just sadness to a combination of grief and helplessness that only intensified when I went on a teen tour to Eastern Europe in my senior year of high school. We traveled across Europe and learned about Jewish history in Prague, Germany, and Poland before visiting various concentration camps. I was far from home, but the ghosts of my ancestors were right beside me. A chill ran down my spine, knowing I wasn't alone. There was death in the air, haunting my every step.

As I trudged forward on the rocky pebbles, I couldn't raise my gaze to meet friends around me. Our mostly lighthearted trip was suddenly serious. Although we were all Jewish, we were from all over the country with a wide array of knowledge and experiences. Somehow, we each made the decision to come together and learn about the history of European Jewry and the Holocaust.

Majdanek concentration camp had not changed in seventy years. The German soldiers did not have time to destroy it as the war came to an end, so it remained the same as it once stood. Overnight, the memorial could be turned back into a fully functioning concentration camp. The wooden barracks were worn and weathered, but they stood firmly in place. Barbed wire surrounded the overgrown grass, marking the end of the prison. My family was not in Majdanek, but I couldn't help feeling like I had been there before. It was eerie walking through the still-standing camp, feeling the haunting presence of those who had their lives ripped away from them.

For my entire life, I always knew about the Holocaust. There is no memory of the first time I heard about the six million Jews murdered and that my great-grandparents were among them. It was something deeply ingrained in my sense of self, a constant reminder of how there is no reason other than luck that I am alive. For as long as I can remember, any time someone spoke of the atrocities of the Holocaust, my eyes welled up with tears. I got a knot in my stomach and nausea overcame my entire body.

This time was different. For the first time in my life, I felt absolutely nothing. My entire body was empty. The other members of my group began to cry, but I couldn't. Walking the grounds of the camp felt surreal. My body moved, but I felt like I was observing it from above in some other plane. I could hear the prisoners' footsteps and smell the smoke of burning flesh. They were not allowed to cry or feel. All they could do was keep their heads down and try to survive.

As we walked into the barrack, hair sat in a four-foot pile to the left side. To the right, there were hundreds of shoes. Blocked by a thick pane of glass, I saw the different colors and textures of hair. I envisioned the people to whom it belonged. Among the many pairs of black shoes, a small red pair meant for a child called out to me. It felt like those shoes once belonged to me.

The final stop on our tour was what I dreaded most: the gas chamber. Its wooden stoves were smaller than I expected and there were only two of them. I smelled the faint remnants of smoke, even though I knew they had not been used in many years. My mind couldn't process the grief I felt. I stood in the gas chamber for a long time, longer than the rest of my group members. I was frozen, staring at the furnace and seeing the flames engulf human bodies before turning them to ash. I flinched as I felt the touch of my friend's hand on my shoulder.

"We're going to start walking back," my friend said gently. Her voice cracked slightly, and her eyes were still glossed over from crying.

My mind had yet to release its cloudy daze, but the long morning was finally coming to an end.

As I boarded the bus, I heard laughter. The other teenagers on my trip were not grandchildren of survivors. They went to the camps and felt sad but were back to their chipper selves the moment we left. As the bus slowly drove away, the outline of the barracks in the distance grew smaller and smaller. When I was finally unable to make out the camp in the distance, the nausea I expected returned. My soul was pulled back into my body and the physical space around me. My stomach ached as if I was punched, and my tears fell down my cheeks. Saying goodbye, I was finally able to mourn. The grief subsided by the end of the day, but the feeling of loss came back in waves. Some days it overtook my entire body for a few minutes, and other days it wouldn't return at all. My trip ended in Israel, a fitting way to bring light to the end of a dark tunnel.

Trips to Israel and going to Jewish sleepaway camp were commonplace in my town growing up. Even though there was a large Jewish population, it didn't make me immune to antisemitism. As I went on to high school, there became a distinction between "Jewish kids" and kids who happened to be Jewish. I was grouped in with the former.

My stomach turned every time someone described me as "so Jewish." My chest tightened and stung, feeling like an insult. I automatically felt the need to go on the defensive, saying, "I'm not even religious. I'm just *culturally* Jewish." I went as far as qualifying my Judaism because I was agnostic. I didn't believe in G-d for the most part, so how could I even be religious? I was secular. I didn't keep Shabbat or go to temple regularly, but I was involved in Jewish organizations and went to Jewish sleepaway camp. Judaism was a huge part in shaping my identity, but I was worried it would completely define it to my peers.

As I walked out of East Brunswick High School for the final time and onto Maryland's campus a few months later, I knew my Jewish identity needed to take a back seat so I could be seen as more than just my religion. At the time, I thought I could segregate my identity, leaving Judaism back in New Jersey. I was unaware of how pervasive my culture was to every fiber of my being.

CHAPTER EIGHT

POPPY

—

As Poppy explored the winding streets of Budapest, his excitement sometimes overtook his grieving. His eyes followed the unique skyline everywhere he walked. Unlike Munkacs, Budapest was split in two by the Danube River, leaving the castle of Buda on the top of a hill as one focal point and the rounded top parliament building as the other. There was nothing to do but make the most of the life he had, so he went out at night to try to enjoy life.

One particular night, he found himself in a lounge. As he walked in, his ears perked up as he heard a familiar melody coming from the piano. He turned to see a woman singing. Her sweet voice wrapped around his heart as it beat louder in rhythm with the music; until the words became familiar and dark, squeezing his heart to a silent beat, forcing him to listen to the song he hadn't heard since before his nightmare began.

"My yiddishe momme," she sang. *My Jewish mom.*

He couldn't hold back anymore as he rushed out onto the dimly lit street. Tears fell down his face as he struggled to gather his breath.

"That was the first time I cried over my mother," Poppy looked away as he spoke, refusing to let me share his pain.

For the next five years he spent in Europe, Poppy held no meaning in his Jewish identity. Holidays once spent with family and friends were no different than any other day during the year. There was no family to host these events or much belief in G-d to celebrate them. Being Jewish nearly killed him, so he pushed that part of his identity to the back burner and focused on celebrating that he was still alive.

As Poppy spoke about this rift between him and religion, I wanted to wrap my arms around him. In my teens and early twenties, I also distanced myself from my Jewish identity. I wanted to live my life without the microaggressions and antisemitism that followed. He understood me on a deeper level than I previously thought.

While he tried to move forward, the past kept pulling him back, begging him to remember. He knew then his past was part of him. What he would do with that knowledge was still uncertain.

As the weeks went by, Poppy traveled. He went to Germany and then Landsberg. He went by himself everywhere, illegally running across the border in the middle of the night. On his way to Germany, he stopped in Bratislava. Then he went to Prague. Everywhere he went, he met some Jewish people, making friends along the way. They were mostly kind and helpful, showing him which border guards were paid off and which way he could get across the border best. Survivors all looked out for one another. They were a new kind of extended family.

After the war, the United Nations set up Displaced Persons camps, known as DP camps, for survivors. They provided food, lodging, and medical care. Poppy went to the DP camps in Germany, and from there he could go wherever he wanted. Without much money or resources, Poppy did a bit of black-market work selling German cameras to Americans.

This was the closest thing he had to a job at the time. The work put a little cash in his pockets. Poppy was free to travel as he pleased. Through his travels, he met a few people from Israel and he worked with the people to help them coordinate for a week or two because he knew Czech and Hebrew.

From Prague, he went to Landsberg and stayed there for a couple of months. He went to the DP camp in the morning to get food. He ran around all day before returning to the camp to eat again. There was nothing for him to do. Every day he woke up, talked to other young people, and did some black-market work. Nobody had a job, and nobody cared what anyone else was doing. He was nineteen years old and had no obligations or responsibilities.

"We were bumming around, what else was there to do?" Poppy asked me as he smiled.

He stayed in Landsberg for a couple of months and then went back to Prague. There, Poppy reunited with Mickey and together they traveled around Europe before settling in Germany at the end of 1945. In Bamberg, Germany, Poppy taught Hebrew to small kids.

They didn't make a lot of money, and all the money they made, they managed to spend. Poppy and Mickey spent money on everything they thought would give them "a good life," from taking girls out to alcohol and food. For a few weeks at a time, they rented apartments across Europe with their black-market money. They spent a small stint in each city before they got bored and moved onto the next.

"When I was in Bamberg, Mickey and I smoked cigarettes and talked with one of the United Nations Relief and Rehabilitation Association officers. He seemed to like us, so he goes, 'UNRRA is opening a new DP camp in Windsheim.' It was in Germany, and they needed people to organize the camp."

The influx of Jews and other people persecuted in the Holocaust was too much for the camps already established. With nowhere else to go and nothing else to do, Poppy and Mickey agreed to help open the new camp.

When they were in Windsheim, Poppy got "very sick in his back," as he described it. The medical diagnosis of his condition was spinal tuberculosis, a side effect of his malnutrition and forced labor in Fünfteichen. As he sat in the medical office, he overheard an American and a German officer. They argued incessantly about the care he needed to receive. The American pushed for surgery, while the German argued a cast would be more effective. The German won and Poppy was put in a full back cast. He laid in that cast for four months. He couldn't do anything but sit and wait for it to come off. Fortunately, after four painful months of waiting, his back was fine when they removed the cast.

In the beginning of 1946, Poppy met his best friends, Herman, "Big" Joe, and "Little" Joe in the Windsheim camp. They spent many nights together drinking, playing cards, and going out on the town. They tried to live and laugh and open their hearts to light after living through so much darkness. This family they created started to mend the gaping hole in his heart. Through word of mouth in the DP camps, Poppy got a message to Bella telling her where he was. Bella came to meet him in Windsheim with a large pregnant stomach. She looked like she was about to burst at the seams. Seeing her pregnant, Poppy saw the rebuilding of his family. He imagined creating new happy memories with a large family seated around his table. This was their future.

Bella fell in love with a man in Budapest and got married. She gave birth to a baby boy, Bobby, within weeks after reuniting with Poppy in Germany. They lived together for two years and then Bella moved to Munich because she was working for JOINT, the Jewish Joint Distribution Committee. She helped provide food, medicine, clothing, and supplies to Holocaust survivors and DP camps facing shortages. Shortly after, she and her family immigrated to the United States.

The life of few responsibilities and constant travel was not sustainable. Poppy always thought he would end up in Israel, but his back made the situation more complicated. It was no longer an option, especially given the impending war. His back could not handle the trauma of fighting. After pressure from Bella begging him to join her and worries about his back taking on the manual farm labor, he finally agreed. In 1950, he decided his future was across the Atlantic Ocean.

"I didn't know where to go, but I knew it was time to move on from the Bohemian life in Europe. I was getting old, and it was enough."

As a refugee, he didn't even have a dollar in his pocket. He was coming to America with only a few items in a small suitcase and the hope to create a future for himself. He spoke a few words of English but knew learning the language wouldn't be his biggest struggle. He already knew seven languages from his childhood and during the war. English would be easy compared to juggling the differences between Hebrew, Hungarian, Czech, Russian, German, Yiddish, and Polish.

Before the war, refugees needed sponsors to guarantee their upkeep in the United States. This way, the government was not responsible for providing for the immigrants; they were only responsible for giving immigrants the right to come to America. Already having family in America gave him preference when applying. He had cousins living in New York for generations, so he was able to write their names and get bumped ahead in line.

To get across the Atlantic, he boarded the *General Blackboard*. "I had no money, so I was told I had to work to pay for my fare. When the time came to volunteer, I chose to help them paint the ice cream box." Poppy looked at me and laughed as he continued, "It was a gimmick. No one actually had to work very hard. In that job, I ate ice cream like it was going out of style."

The water was choppy and rough as they crossed the English Channel. All the passengers got sick, except for Poppy and a few others. But after a week of traveling, the passengers of the *General Blackboard* saw the Statue of Liberty for the first time. They didn't go to Ellis Island like most refugees. They docked at a port in New York City. As he got off the boat, he saw Bella and her husband standing on the dock waiting for him. They smiled and hugged with excitement to be reunited once again. She grinned as she held out an American ice cream cone, clearly proud of her gift.

Poppy smiled, but his stomach was not a happy one. He ran over the side of the dock and vomited. I can't say if his sickness was from the rough and choppy water or eating his weight in ice cream, but it's safe to say he had an aversion to ice cream ever since.

With no money and no plan, he arrived in America. The possibilities for his future were limitless. With his sister by his side, he was ready for whatever challenges came his way.

CHAPTER NINE

MICHELLE

———

Walking onto the University of Maryland's lush green campus was a fresh start. As a freshman in college, no one knew who I was or where I came from. There were no preconceived notions and judgments about religion and background. It was a clean slate for me to be the person who I always wanted to be without being defined by religion as I was for much of my early life. I tried to summon the strength to leave religion behind in order to avoid the stress that led to many years of overwhelming panic and anxiety.

Even through a conscious effort to avoid Chabad and Hillel in the first semester, I was conflicted when it came to Yom Kippur, the holiest day of the Jewish year. Yom Kippur was a fast day where I spent the entire day in services growing up. I never enjoyed the services aspect of the holiday, but being surrounded by my friends and family made it bearable. The best part was the big party my parents would host to break the fast, but it wasn't an option this year. Rosh Hashanah fell on a weekend, so it was easy enough to go home, but this was the middle of the week. There was no easy way to escape back to my family.

There wasn't really a decision to make. Of course, I would email my professors and miss class to fast on Yom Kippur.

My parents would never forgive me if I didn't. The bigger question was what to do during the day. As easily as I could have watched *One Tree Hill* in my room all day, I felt guilt nagging me. I knew the right thing to do was to go to services and sit there, but it wasn't that simple. Memories of being ostracized growing up haunted me. I couldn't fall back into the same pattern.

I knew the only person I could get an honest opinion from was Poppy. The night before Yom Kippur I called him to get advice on my dilemma.

"Why are you asking me? I haven't been to services in years," he replied.

I rolled my eyes. "I don't want to be seen as just another Jewish girl in college."

"At the end of the day it's your choice, but there's no harm in going for a bit. You can always leave early. It would make your mom happy to hear you went."

My traditional mother always expected my brother and I to attend Jewish holiday services. She often went not only on the high holidays, but sometimes on regular Saturdays as well. In Judaism my mom found community and enjoyed going to temple. Religion in the traditional sense was significantly more important to her than it was to either me or Poppy.

He always knew the right thing to say and how to guide my moral compass. I ultimately decided to go for an hour. When I arrived, I saw a friend from my high school youth group, and we sat talking for most of the service. In Judaism, everyone talks at services and it is a social experience. Having someone else there made time fly faster than sitting and staring at the walls alone. It was bearable. In compromising, I found a middle ground. That night, my friend and I gorged ourselves on dining hall bagels and ice cream. It wasn't breaking the fast at my parents, but I had someone to share the experience with.

The first semester flew by, and I started to get my bearings. The classes were not particularly stressful or difficult, but I was still uneasy. None of the people I met seemed to be people I could see myself being friends with in the long term. I was still looking for a place to call home in the large undergraduate student body. Right before Thanksgiving break, a flyer caught my eye. Its vibrant colors were warm and inviting. I began to smile.

Panhellenic Sorority Recruitment: Find Your Home.

I always thought about what it would be like to join a sorority, surrounded by people who shared the same values. I wanted a support structure and a way to make new friends and meet new people. Greek life seemed like the perfect way to do that.

Finally, the days of Panhellenic Recruitment arrived. I didn't know what to expect other than needing to dress nicely and talk to each sorority house over the span of the weekend, tracking which ones I connected with and which ones I didn't. My recently dyed blonde hair was neatly curled and held still by a mountain of hair spray. My face was painted in makeup, but just enough it looked almost natural, and my outfit was carefully selected to make a good impression without looking like I was trying too hard.

As I walked from house to house, I was paired up with bubbly and friendly girls. My outgoing personality thrived on meeting so many new people and playing geography to find common interests and connections. The first weekend flew by as I met person after person, searching for where I could see myself for the next four years. The names and faces of all the people I spoke to blurred together. My list of potential homes kept shrinking smaller and smaller as I ranked each conversation I had, hoping the girls I spoke to felt the same way and requested me to return.

The final round of recruitment narrowed my choices down to two houses that couldn't be more different. As I walked into Alpha Chi Omega, I felt the passion of the women around me for their philanthropy: domestic violence awareness. Each woman I spoke to seemed self-assured and empowered as they spoke about the way their sisters in Alpha Chi supported them to reach their potential. My conversations were thought-provoking and interesting, about greater societal issues and the importance of educating others and enabling them to make a positive change. They were all different personalities but brought together by shared values. I walked out of the house, uncertain about the choice I would make.

As I walked across fraternity row, my mind raced. I entered the doors of Alpha Epsilon Phi, a Jewish sorority. Full of "nice Jewish girls" with similar backgrounds to me, I was at home in this house. Each conversation was effortless and light. The girls I spoke to had friends that went to the same sleepaway camp as me growing up and they participated in Jewish youth groups like I did well into high school. There was an innate comfort in being surrounded by people "just like me." With that comfort and homogeneity, I felt my ever-present recurring shame. I was reminded of the feelings I felt far too often growing up when confronting my Judaism.

The last round of recruitment came and went. My mind was back and forth as I grappled with what I was truly looking for. I wasn't sure if I wanted to branch out or be comforted by what was familiar. This was my opportunity to be whoever I wanted to be. I had the opportunity to meet new people and grow or I could stay stagnant in a bubble, sheltered from anyone with a different background.

Standing at the bus stop outside of fraternity row, I suddenly burst into tears. The weight of a decision that could decide my entire college experience was too much for me. I felt lost and helpless. When I entered the Stamp Student Union, it was time for me to make an important choice. I needed to choose between the person I grew up as or the person I aspired to be. With that, my decision was made. I pushed myself to grow, even if that future was uncertain and uncomfortable. But that didn't mean fate would agree with me. With mutual selection, I would have to choose a house and they would also have to choose me. As I handed in my rankings, my heart pounded. I was uncertain Alpha Chi was the right choice.

On bid day, the anticipation was high. We each sat on the smooth wooden floor inside the Stamp ballroom. I took slow, deep breaths to calm my racing heart. As I closed my eyes, I tried to drown out the hushed whispers of girls anxious for their results. We each would receive a letter containing our destination and landing in Greek Life. We waited as the president of Greek Life gave us a speech. I was too distracted to follow what she was saying.

Did I make the right choice yesterday? Maybe I was wrong.

A part of me hoped my gut instinct was wrong and I should have stayed with what I knew. I was full of doubts and goose bumps lined my arms. The letter arrived in my hands. My future was written inside of that sealed envelope. My breathing couldn't calm my nerves any longer. I warily slipped my finger underneath the seal, careful not to rip the precious document inside. It was almost as if harming the single piece of paper would void the entire process. As I pulled the card out, three Greek letters stared back at me.

Alpha Chi Omega

My heart flooded with delight for the next four years. My smile spread across my face, unable to hold in my excitement. I jumped up and down with the other girls in my group who were as happy and relieved as I was to get their first choice. I ran over to the Alpha Chi Omega group and threw my new T-shirt over my head. I could shape myself into anyone I wanted to be. It was a conscious choice to define my identity on my own terms.

Joining a sorority wasn't as simple as I expected. At first, it was instant friends and a place of belonging. I expected my stress about not fitting in to disappear. As the rest of the year went on, the groups began to downsize. This uneasiness about not having a specific friend group only intensified when it came to determining who would move into the house the following school year.

My GPA was very high from first semester, but the house had only a few open spots. I was put on a waiting list until older girls made their final decisions of whether they would move in. My perpetual waiting lasted for weeks. I reached out time and time again to the head of housing, hearing no updates. All the other girls seemed to make plans. Once again, there was no place for me. The stress continued to compound, and my panic attacks increased. The worst was yet to come. One night, the recurring nightmare from my childhood decided to make an appearance, undoubtedly brought on by my increased stress.

The nightmare was usually fuzzy and vague, but it always started at night. I was hidden in a room or a closet inside of a large building that reminded me of a hotel. There were long hallways and someone was looking for me. I heard the people get closer and closer. They walked quickly down the halls, knocked strongly on doors, and violently went through people's rooms.

I knew if I stayed where I was, they would find me, so I needed to start moving. I snuck out of my room right before they turned the corner and I started running down the hallways, sometimes slipping into other rooms. Usually, it was a stone building with secret stairwells and passages I ran down. I hid periodically, checking to see if they followed me or if anyone saw me.

At some point, I always ended up in the center area. It looked like a lobby and there were other people there. At this point, it was rainy or misty and cold. Some people yelled while others were sobbing. I always saw a mother with her arms wrapped around her young daughter standing in front of her. Her fear was written clearly across her raised eyebrows and slightly open mouth. Then, they were marched away from the building with little or no belongings.

Finally, I woke up.

It never occurred to me that this was anything more than a nightmare. The next day, I told my friend Rachel about my recurring dream. From an outside perspective, this nightmare painted a clear picture. She automatically knew the men I was running and hiding from were Nazis and the people getting hoarded into the center of the building and marched away were Jews. The recurring nightmare I brushed off my entire life suddenly took on new meaning.

CHAPTER TEN

MICHELLE

———

Even as I began to embrace my new identity in college, the shame I felt growing up was not without reason. The reason for anxiety and shame surrounding my identity was deeply rooted in the antisemitism my family and I experienced throughout our lives. I was at a school with a high Jewish population, but that did not insulate me from the reality of antisemitism.

My junior year of college, I lived in my sorority house where the walls were thin enough to hear conversations clearly, so a slammed door left an echo reverberating through the halls. I closed my textbook from late night studying and tried to determine where the loud sound came from. After the slam of the door, I heard quiet crying. I knew the sound couldn't have come from too far away. I followed the crying to find my friend Liv sitting in her bed, her face stained with tears. Her makeup was smeared on her cheeks and her dark hair was tied away from her face in two messy braids. She looked feeble in her oversized T-shirt. I was concerned why the strong confident woman I knew was gone. I approached her meekly, hoping not to startle her.

"Are you okay?" I asked.

Her facial expression made it apparent that she wasn't. It was a combination between sadness, confusion, and anger. I could not tell which was the strongest of her conflicting emotions. Her blue eyes were glazed over and red from sobbing. She blew her nose and took a deep breath, trying to compose herself before recounting in detail the horrifying events of her night.

Our sorority was having a party with a fraternity as it normally did on Thursday nights. The theme was "highlighter party," which consisted of everyone wearing white T-shirts and walking around with highlighter markers drawing on each other. The dark house had a black light to make the drawings even more vibrant and bright. A fraternity member approached one of our sisters, Mel. She had blonde straight hair and piercing blue eyes. He began to draw on her shoulder. When she looked down, a big yellow swastika was on her. Her demeanor quickly changed from happy to serious as she berated him. She was never one to mess with. As she yelled at him, the member apologetically crossed the drawing out and ran away.

Not even ten minutes later, the same member approached Liv. Her warm and amicable attitude always drew others to her. She was the life of the party, always dancing and chatting with a million new friends every time she went out. He spoke with her briefly before his yellow highlighter touched the back of her already full T-shirt. As he lifted his marker, he smiled and let out a laugh before running away into the dark crowd of people. One of her friends whispered in her ear that the boy just drew a swastika on her back.

Unlike Mel, Liv was half-Jewish. She recently began to connect with her Jewish identity after meeting so many proud Jews in college. Our sorority was not nationally Jewish, but there were many Jewish members like any organization at the University of Maryland. After seeing this symbol marking her shirt, she could not contain herself. She was so appalled, disgusted, and upset by what happened, she left the event in tears. She ran home crying and threw her shirt in the garbage can the second she walked in the door.

She lowered her head as she spoke. "It was terrifying. I...I just don't know what—" She couldn't even finish her sentence. Her forehead creased as she tightly shut her eyes.

"You need to report this to someone at the university," I said gently.

"I will," she responded. Her voice cracked as she added, "But that will have to wait for tomorrow. For tonight, I just want to go to bed and forget this happened."

In the following weeks, the incident was reported, and the University conducted an investigation. With witnesses sharing testimony and strong evidence to support the case, the boy was removed from his fraternity. It was an appropriate procedure and within a matter of weeks most of the community went back to normal.

Everyone continued with their lives but I couldn't shake the anxiety that persisted with me everywhere I went. I lost my appetite and was too overwhelmed to socialize with any of my friends in the common room. This incident was not a surprising event. For years, I sat at desks with swastikas engraved into them. The symbols of hate burned into my memory never left me but were seen as a joke to so many others. This was supposed to be a safe space for young adults to be who they are and grow. If this was happening at a place like Maryland, with a vibrant Jewish population, it could only be worse at other universities. The impact of this act of intolerance had wide-ranging implications. I knew I couldn't stay silent.

Two months after the fraternity party incident, I applied to be a "Terp Talk" speaker. This TED talk-style event gave students the opportunity to bring their ideas to life. I knew by distancing myself from my religion, I was leaving other Jewish students alone to be targeted. No one would stand up for us if we would not stand up for ourselves. It was my obligation to stop letting others feel the same shame I avoided. I needed to share the power of words. I shared the story of my friend, but also of the larger societal microaggressions used by many daily.

Jews are not alone in experiencing acts of intolerance and violence, but these small biases led to millions of Europeans looking the other way while the calculated attempt of eliminating an entire ethnicity occurred. Even if American Jews begin to forget where they come from, there will always be those who will not. In Germany, before World War II, many Jews were incredibly secular. They defined themselves as German first and Jewish second, but the German people did not forget they were Jews. If we do not choose to actively remember our history, we can soon begin to fall into the same traps that have harmed us in every generation.

The biggest theme I wanted to get across in this speech was that words are not just words. Words are reflections of ideas, and ideas then turn into actions. Nearly twenty of my friends and acquaintances came to the event to support me. My mom drove down from New Jersey just to hear me speak. Once I finished, I was quickly surrounded by the large group, congratulating me on making my voice heard. I don't know if my words impacted anyone listening, but there was a small piece of me who thought I could make a difference.

October 29, 2018, is a vivid day in my memory. Two days after the Tree of Life shooting in Pittsburgh, Pennsylvania, a vigil was held at McKeldin Mall at the University of Maryland. This vigil was meant to commemorate the victims of the shooting. One of my friends, Jake, was asked to speak about the Pittsburgh Jewish community he grew up in. I walked out of my club meeting like any other Monday evening. It was fifteen minutes prior to the vigil, and I stopped to look over the vast darkness covering the people on the mall. It was never well-lit at night, but that night it felt especially dark. I could hardly see a few feet in front of me and I stopped. A familiar feeling overcame me—anxiety. My body felt like it was in overdrive with fight-or-flight response.

I thought of how easy it would be for someone who wanted to harm people to go there. I didn't often think like this, but it was a large crowd of Jewish people coming together to mourn the loss of members of our people and our community. My mind was overtaken with thoughts of how easy it would be for us to become a target. Campus police officers lined the outside of the grass, but that wouldn't prevent someone from walking onto the public space and doing whatever they wanted. My mind flashed to images of hiding on the ground as shots fired. They seemed real and fear seeped in.

I pushed myself to walk onto the grass. I knew this was exactly where I needed to be, even with the fear of impending doom. Among the sea of indistinguishable faces waiting to hear a comforting voice, I was alone. A finger tapped my shoulder, causing the hairs on my arm to stand up as I unintentionally jumped. As I spun around, I exhaled when I saw a familiar face of my dormmate from freshman year. It was such a vulnerable feeling being there, in public, without protection.

I listened intently as I heard Jake approach the microphone. His words resonated with me deeply as he spoke about the community he grew up in and the places and people he knew. I saw myself in him as he spoke. It occurred to me how easily it could have been me, my family, my friends, my community that experienced something so tragic and traumatic. I never felt like that before, afraid to go somewhere as a Jew.

The Tree of Life shooting shattered the image I had of my temple being a safe place for me to go. For years leading up to that day, police officers stood outside in the parking lot for the high holidays. Over the years, police presence increased to a weekly event. This was meant to keep us safe and ward off dangers. It always seemed like a precautionary measure to have them there. This was the first time I realized what their constant attendance meant. It was not just precautionary. They were there not for if someone came to harm us, but rather when that day came.

Even in a country as great as America, conspiracy theories run wild, blaming Jewish space lasers and labeling successful Jewish businesspeople as puppeteers behind the scenes. How can we so easily forget who we are, when the rest of the world most certainly will not?

The shots fired in Pittsburgh echoed through the halls of every synagogue in America. They brought gravity and reality into the world we live in. Antisemitism is not some outdated idea of the past. A shudder went down my spine as the dark realization I tried to avoid set in. It is still not safe to be a Jew, even in America.

CHAPTER ELEVEN

MICHELLE

The darkness felt like it was consuming me from the inside out. I started to fall into it, allowing it to engulf me. In the distance, I heard a weak sound calling me out from the darkness.

As I heard the quiet beeping of my alarm clock, it seemed fainter than usual, almost like it was muffled under a pillow. My morning grogginess washed over me. Weighed down by what I expected was a poor night's sleep, I put on my comfiest sweats, made my coffee, and headed across campus.

Dragging my heavy legs to Van Munching Hall, I noticed my gait was slower than usual as students passed me on either side. My stomach ached as I tried to sip down the piping liquid from my mug, hoping the caffeine would jolt my body awake and keep me moving through the day. Unfortunately, this was not the case. I could barely drink as nausea took over. As I collapsed in my seat, the heaviness of my legs creeped up through my entire body. My heart ached and tears swelled in my eyes. I had no thoughts, no emotions—just emptiness from my mind perpetuating down to my core.

This wasn't the first time this feeling overtook my body. It happened sporadically throughout my young adult life, usually lasting for a few hours here and there before something snapped me out of the daze. This time was different. It felt deeper. The tiredness of my body begged me to go back home and curl up in my bed, but I didn't know if my legs were strong enough to carry me back across campus. Disinterestedly, I followed my daily routine, expecting to snap back to my chipper self from one of the sights or sounds around me. I trudged through the motions, sitting in one seat then the other for my classes for the day. The faint words of my professors were muted by the emptiness that seemed to consume everything around me.

When the class day was finally over, it took every ounce of strength in my mind to carry my body back to the sorority house. Lunchtime was in full swing as twenty girls crowded the kitchen ordering lunch from the chef. Their loud conversations made my ears pound. The smell of tater tots that usually overtook the house at lunch made my stomach do backflips, so I sulked back into my small bedroom for solitude.

The next morning, the weight holding me down only intensified. My phone buzzed full of missed messages I still did not have the energy to answer. I was stuck while the whole world moved on around me. I wasn't myself, instead I was a marionette doll with someone else controlling my strings.

The next few days all blurred together. After a mandatory sorority board meeting, I went back to my friend Reagan's apartment with our friend, Rachel. Reagan's cute puppy was the last bit of hope I had for someone cheering me up. Rachel pulled me aside and asked, "What's wrong? You don't seem like yourself."

I shrugged and whispered, "I don't know." My voice cracked as my gaze lowered to the floor. That was the closest I came to forming a full sentence in nearly three days. My chest got heavy and tears swelled up in my eyes. I knew making eye contact would open the floodgates on this mysterious storm cloud controlling me.

"I don't want this to come out the wrong way, but you should think about seeing someone. I think that could help you," Rachel said. Her normally cheery and upbeat demeanor was calm and level. Pained concern was written all over her face, her brows furrowed slightly, and her eyes had hints of fear for what my reaction would be.

The water I was holding spilled, and I suddenly became aware of my trembling hands. The heat drained from my body and I was paralyzed. I tried to speak, but no sound came out. The only thing I could do was nod my head and mouth, "All right."

It was that moment I decided to look for a therapist. Less than two weeks later, I was en route to my first appointment with Dustin Menick.

My heart pounded in my ears as my car rolled down the tree-lined streets of Bethesda. The roads were clean and newly paved. I managed to parallel park and finagle my blue Subaru into a large spot. The car was about a foot away from the curb when I turned it off, but I was too wired to adjust my poor attempt at parallel parking. My hands shook as I inserted quarters into the meter. I felt like lead was dropped in my stomach.

I could just turn around and go home right now.

But I came too far to turn around. I knew I couldn't keep living the way I had been, fearful of my anxiety attacks. Instead of improving between high school and college, they only intensified and became more frequent. Somewhere deep down, it was clear that trying to process the aftermath of my depressive episode was not something I could do on my own. I braced myself for the worst. I found the name Menick and pressed the small buzzer beneath it to indicate I arrived ten minutes early. Punctuality was always my strong suit. My parents drilled into me the importance of punctuality, leading to my perpetual fear of being late. I sat in the empty waiting room and zoned out, scrolling mindlessly through my phone. As Dustin Menick popped her head out the doorway to call me into her office, I received a text from my best friend Emma.

"You can do this. Call me after."

I walked through the door into a small office. I looked at the couch as I pictured a stereotypical scene from a movie starring me. The scene would probably look like me lying down talking through my whole life, from birth to the present, as Dustin furiously took notes on her clipboard, and then me walking away feeling cured. This was not reality.

I was taken by surprise, not only because my therapist was a young woman instead of the middle-aged man I pictured in my head but also because the office looked comfortable and cozy instead of sterile. Still, I sat uncomfortably on the sandy beige couch. I fiddled in my seat, not knowing whether to sit up or lie down. I settled on remaining seated as Dustin sat in an oversized blue armchair across from me. There was no clipboard like I pictured, just a small notebook placed on a side table that she didn't open. Her blonde hair and soft smile were inviting, but my heart pounded. If she could hear it from her chair, she gave no indication. My eyes darted from the chair to small pieces of artwork to the little side table next to me, trying to make sense of my strange new surroundings.

"Hi Michelle, I'm Dusty. Let's start by telling me why you came to see me today." Her voice was gentle with a little bit of raspiness. Her tone was upbeat and familiar, like a friend catching up after a long absence.

She was straight to the point. I knew there was no reason not to be, but I couldn't help but feel my face flush. My embarrassment and discomfort made me shuffle from side to side in my seat as I searched for the right words to describe what occurred a few weeks prior. As I spoke, the tears rushed out of my eyes like a waterfall.

"I'm sorry. I don't even know why I'm crying right now," I sputtered.

"Take your time. There are tissues next to you if you need them. Besides, people cry here all the time."

I somehow pulled myself together to explain my depressive episode. I explained how I didn't even know what it was, let alone why it happened. She listened intently and asked questions to gather background. As a naturally open person, I felt myself going through my family history more than my own life story. I shared details of my large family and my grandfather's survival of the Holocaust. I continued to explain through my family dynamic of strong individuals who all overcame so much on their own and the "pull yourself up by your bootstraps and move forward" mentality. Suddenly, I shut my mouth.

"But none of this is their fault," I said matter-of-factly.

"Why do you say that?" she asked, gently nudging for more details.

"I have the best family in the world. They didn't do anything to make me like this."

Before I knew it, an hour flew by. She thanked me as I walked out the door.

"Thank you for coming, Michelle. Let me know if you want to schedule another appointment."

I rushed to my car, my face sticky and immobile from my dried tears. I was nauseous and my stomach turned as I stepped back into the safety of my car. I thought one therapy session would fix me, not make me feel even more hopeless.

I didn't want some stranger judging the wrongdoings of the greatest people I knew.

They always blame the parents, I thought, convinced I would never return to the vulnerable state I felt in the small room. Vulnerability was a feeling I had avoided for most of my life. It was the antithesis to the empowered and independent woman I always forced myself to be. Even from a young age, I was a high achiever with a constant aim for perfection. Expressing my feelings of self-doubt, imposter syndrome, and anxiety out loud made them real. It meant I was too weak to handle my own mind on my own. I had already talked myself out of going back for another therapy session. As I was about to leave, my phone started to vibrate. I answered and started to breathe as I heard Emma's voice. I didn't realize I was holding my breath.

"How did it go?" she asked.

"Honestly, I don't think it's for me." I gave her the rundown of my session: my uncontrollable crying, oversharing of my family history, and the immense discomfort I felt throughout. "My family doesn't go to therapy. They handle things on their own, why can't I?"

"This was only your first session. It can be really uncomfortable sharing with someone for the first time. I know it was for me too. Promise me you will go again, and if you still don't want to do this, then fine. It's a slow process and takes time to get used to. I think it could really help you if you let it."

Somewhere deep down, I knew Emma was right. Not only was she my best friend since I was three years old, but Emma also struggled with mental health and saw firsthand how her grandmother dealt with the guilt and pain of surviving the Holocaust. Emma and her family were going to therapy for years at this point and knew much more than I did about its benefits. Somehow, after the thirty-minute drive back to campus, she had completely shifted my perspective. She knew me better than I did myself and had a way of convincing me when she really pushed.

As I pulled my car into its spot, I reached my conclusion. It didn't matter what a therapist thought of my family but rather what I knew to be true. I have been gifted with the most loving and supportive people in the world. Just because they rarely talked about their feelings didn't mean that I couldn't. I wanted to be strong enough to handle my issues on my own, but maybe getting help was exactly what I needed.

After that conversation with Emma, I continued to see Dusty to the present day. As our visits became regular, I slowly opened up and felt comfortable talking about my emotions. I analyzed what triggered my anxiety and why I perpetually needed to overachieve and be independent from relying on anyone else. We discussed why I didn't want to burden anyone else in my life by needing help or support. Within the first few sessions, Dusty brought up the notion of generational trauma. I had never heard the term before, but I assumed it was a psychologist's way of blaming family for children with mental health problems. Nonetheless, the word was deeply etched in my mind, begging for understanding.

Generational trauma. Generational trauma. What does that even mean? The thought looped around my head, gnawing at me as I tried to rationalize its implications.

The Holocaust and Judaism have always been part of my identity, for better or for worse. While it is still a young field, researchers have been conducting studies assessing anxiety, depression, and PTSD in Holocaust survivors and their descendants. Most of them found significantly higher rates of these mental health disorders in descendants of Holocaust survivors than their peers without family history of trauma (DeAngelis, 2019). Generational trauma and its biological aftereffects transcend generations.

A 1988 study conducted by *The Canadian Journal of Psychiatry* found that grandchildren of Holocaust survivors were overrepresented by about 300 percent in psychiatric care referrals. This research doesn't just stop at diagnosing illnesses but continues to epigenetic transmission. According to *The American Journal of Psychiatry*, Heather Bader and her colleagues found the same changes in the location of a stress-related gene and levels of a stress-related receptor in Holocaust survivors and their children linked to depression and PTSD. These were not comparable to the control group of people who had not experienced such trauma (2014).

The idea of generational trauma then became more of a combination of nature and nurture. This topic caused me to take a step back and look at the experiences in my life influenced by this combination of my DNA and the experiences I had. It was time for me to start piecing together the components that made me into the person I am today, but what right did I have to complain about my privileged upbringing in upper-middle-class suburbia? Whatever trauma I had experienced could never be compared to the horrors of the Holocaust.

CHAPTER TWELVE

MICHELLE

———

Biweekly sessions with Dusty became something I looked forward to instead of a chore. While my crying barely subsided, it was a release of pent-up stress and energy. Every session brought a new insight into whatever stress I dealt with and created a safe space to analyze and dissect it. There was no judgment.

Many sessions revolved around my stress from school, but the recurring theme was my perfectionism and anxiety. Coincidentally, these issues went hand in hand. The anxiety caused by my perfectionism sometimes paralyzed me into not getting a task done at all. Fear was my biggest hindrance, causing me to avoid anything pushing me out of my comfort zone.

When we talked about identity, my self-image stayed conflicted. I would cry and tell her the same repeated line and stories I told her before.

"I love my family and my culture, but I need to keep that part of myself hidden or I will never be accepted."

As we continued to talk, I noticed that even in a non-religious sorority and on a diverse campus, the people around me were overwhelmingly Jewish. Somehow, Jewish people continued to end up in my circle.

As April rolled around, I knew Passover was coming up. I had no way to get myself the three-hour ride home in the middle of the week to celebrate the holiday that was the most near and dear to my mother's heart. It was never one of my favorite holidays, but the thought of being away when my entire family was together was nearly unbearable. Then, at lunch as I ate my standard peanut butter and honey sandwich, my friend Jacob asked me what I was doing for Passover.

"I'm not sure. Because of when it falls this year, I can't go home." My voice was full of disappointment as I recounted everyone and everything I was missing.

"You should come to my house!" My gaze focused on Jacob and my heart was warmed by this thoughtful gesture. Jacob grew up in a similar level of religious observance as I did. He understood the importance of being with family on this holiday.

Just like that, I was brought into another family for one of the most sacred meals of the year. I walked into his Rockville home and his family welcomed me as if I had been coming to their seders for years. The table was small with only about twelve seats around it, but I was relieved to be part of it. As soon as we finished the reading and prepared to eat, I stood up and walked to the kitchen. His mother smiled in surprise for the extra help. She thanked me as she handed me bowl after bowl of chicken soup. Then, we cleared the table and placed dishes in the sink.

The meal was different than I was used to. There wasn't an assortment of ten kugels to choose from, nor were there any Hungarian twists on the meat dishes like Poppy would make, but it was Passover nonetheless. I wondered what my grandfather was doing in New Jersey, who was serving his food and singing the four questions while I was with another family.

After dinner, we took a long walk to talk and digest our meals. It was a beautiful crisp night without a single cloud in the sky. There was a slight April breeze, but not enough to make us cold. I looked up to see the stars and an overwhelming sense of peace washed over me. This was the feeling of belonging I was missing.

We finished our walk and said our goodbyes. As we drove back to campus, something felt different. The peace from that walk stayed with me.

"Thank you so much for inviting me. You don't know how much this meant to me."

Jacob smiled as he responded jokingly, "My mom wouldn't shut up about you. She was so happy to have someone help her serve. You're welcome back at our house anytime."

Judaism somehow found its way back into my secular world. As I explored my long list of interests, like reading, music, and sports, I thought back to the joyful parts of my Jewish childhood equally important in my identity. Judaism was no longer the defining trait of my identity, but a part of the mosaic that made up my life. To ignore and hide that section would take away from the beauty of the picture, just as ignoring or hiding my Judaism would take away from the complexity of my character.

As I began to come to terms with defining my Jewish identity, I no longer specifically kept myself away from Jewish organizations, especially after finding out one would pay me just to attend a class once a week. The learning fellowship through the MEOR organization ignited something in me that increased my curiosity about Jewish education.

The sun went down and left an eerie feeling on Old Town College Park. Through the foggy dusk I could see the letters TEPhi on the side of a darkened brick building. I heard

MEOR was in a shared building with the fraternity TEP, but I had never been there before. Unsure of where to enter, I slowly walked around the dark brick building. The last thing I wanted was to walk into a fraternity house when I expected to attend a learning seminar. I walked up the front steps skeptically before the front door swung open wide. I sighed with relief as the familiar face of the young spokeswoman smiled back at me.

"Michelle! I am so excited for you to join us. I even baked my world-famous brownies this week to start off our program!" DJ squealed with delight as she ushered me through the door.

I awkwardly thanked her and found a seat in the second of three rows. Automatically, I looked down at my phone, hoping to avoid the awkwardness of not knowing anyone before the lecture began. For DJ, that was not an option. She grabbed my arm and walked me around, introducing me to one person after the other. This was a community she was part of and welcomed me into even though we hardly knew each other. My heart raced and my jaw tightened in this unfamiliar place with so many new faces around me. I smiled politely as she introduced me, knowing I wouldn't remember any of the people I just met, and quickly returned to my seat as the speaker walked up to the front of the room.

A young woman confidently stood before me. As she spoke, my shoulders came away from my ears. My jaw, clenched with my teeth grinding together, softened. Her energy and passion were invigorating.

What I expected to be a lecture on Judaism was actually the compelling and sad life story of a mother struggling with raising a child who had severe mental problems. Somehow, she found meaning and comfort through the Jewish religion and teachings. A story one expected to be tragic was actually a story of hope and meaning. She said two words I have continued to repeat to this day: *Hakarat Hatov*. Those words were like a beck and call guiding me. They were familiar on my tongue, like they were always meant to be there. The corners of my mouth curled upward as I relaxed into my seat. I knew I was in a safe place.

In Hebrew, Hakarat Hatov is the word "gratitude," but its direct translation is far more insightful. Recognize the good. No matter the situation, there is always a silver lining and something good to see from it. Judaism has resilience I often overlooked. My grandfather embodied this more than anyone.

From the trauma of the past, there is a light in the future. From that point on, I found new understanding in what it meant to be Jewish. I loved attending class week after week and it no longer became about the small stipend I would receive in the end. There was so much more to Judaism than what Hebrew school taught me. There were important life lessons and testaments that could be applied to experiences I was having each and every day.

As the next four years passed, I slowly became more comfortable expressing my religion without resentment. I created little reminders of the parts of Judaism I loved growing up. I brought food back and shared it with friends after holidays. Once I had my own kitchen, I even spent Purim with Jacob, making hamantaschen and delivering them to different people I knew around campus. It was my tribute to my days spent with my mom delivering mishloach manot.

Purim has always been one of my favorite holidays. Ever since I was a little girl, I baked hamantaschen and made mishloach manot with my mom. Mishloach manot are gift bags traditionally given on Purim filled with hamantaschen, candy, fruit, and pennies.

She and I spent hours in the kitchen making dough and, using a glass, we cut out small circles to fill with every type of filling imaginable. Her delicate touch somehow always prevented the dough from sticking to the counter. From chocolate chip, to jelly, prune, and poppy seed, we filled the centers and then pinched the corners, making the iconic triangle shape. Every year the recipe changed, hoping that one day we would find the perfect dough. Small circles lined our long kitchen counters and the black granite turned grey with the layer of flour coating it. Once the cookies were out of the oven, we filled tray after tray organizing by what was contained in each delicious center.

Everyone we knew had a favorite flavor, so we labeled the bags with individual names to ensure there was an extra touch of love. I sat at the table affixing little labels onto the bags saying "Happy Purim from the Weinfelds" before stuffing them full of sweets. Then, my mom and I sat down with our handwritten list, mapping out the most efficient way to deliver all thirty of the bags across town.

We always made extra because along the way my mom would inevitably exclaim, "I can't believe we forgot to give a bag to this person! We have to drop one off there. They are hardly even out of the way," even if that person's house added another fifteen minutes to our trip.

As we pulled up to a house, I ran around the back of the car and found the labeled bag. Grabbing it, I rushed up to the front door, placing it gently to make sure the cookies didn't crumble. I rang the doorbell and sprinted back into the car. We repeated this process over and over again until every house was crossed off our list. One year, my brother and I thought it would be a better idea to deliver in our neighborhood by biking around and dropping them off. With no baskets on our bicycles and the bags hitting onto our wheels, it was a complete failure. We reluctantly returned home, disappointed that our environmentally conscious effort was a disaster.

When I called Poppy to tell him of our defeat, he laughed as he spoke. "When I was your age, I would go on my bike from house to house delivering mishloach manot. They were a big thing where I grew up. The hamantaschen were similar to the ones you make, but we used some different fillings."

The night before Purim his family made mishloach manot and they even mailed them to Poppy's father's family far away in the Carpathian Mountains. During Purim day, they schlepped on the bike, going door to door, trying not to drop the baskets, and seemingly doing a better job than my brother and I did on our attempt. Poppy's mother made them for a lot of people and Poppy served as the delivery boy. They sent a lot of mishloach manot and received a lot in return. They sometimes regifted them though, sending someone else's to other people if they didn't like what was in it. The whole community came together to participate.

This tradition epitomized exactly what Judaism was for me growing up. It combined my love for food and baking with spending time with my mom and being part of a community. The excitement I got whenever someone dropped a basket at our door never failed to make me smile. Even after we finally moved away from my childhood home, my mom and I still made the trip back together. The list grew shorter and the distance more confined to our old neighborhood, but the sentiment remained exactly the same. Going away to college and thinking back to this tradition reminded me of the importance of community. Through traditions surrounded by food, I remembered where I came from and where I was going.

CHAPTER THIRTEEN

POPPY

———

"The ship let us off on a Wednesday. It was a long way there, but Bella and Willie took me right to the East Bronx. Our cousin owned an apartment there and he told me I could stay as long as I needed. The cheap rent didn't hurt either," Poppy chuckled as he shared. He was noticeably more comfortable talking about what life was like after he arrived in America.

Two days after arriving in New York, Poppy's friend from the DP camps called the apartment. He heard about Poppy's recent trip through the ever-present gossip chain.

"So this guy called me and said, 'You need a job for a few days? We need help working in a factory for uniforms.' They were like what nurses wear. I went, what else am I doing? So, I said why not?" He brushed his hand to the side, indicating his nonchalance.

Saturday morning, he woke up early and went to the factory. He helped his friend out, and on Sunday night the foreman of the factory asked him if he wanted a job. He noticed Poppy's strong work ethic in his two-day stint at the factory. Once again, Poppy's response was why not. He had just arrived in America but didn't realize opportunities would come so soon. He lived the last five years with no responsibilities, but now was the time to start building his future.

He ended up staying at that job for ten years, doing whatever work his boss requested. Some days he worked on the assembly line, other days he dealt directly with customers or even drove deliveries himself. Through those ten years, he slowly gained the respect of the boss and managers. They weren't fond of refugees but, through hard work, Poppy became a top manager. They never formally gave him the title "Shipping Manager," but he had all the power and responsibilities. It wasn't the job or the life he envisioned for himself, but he made the most of it. He had no idea where he was going. He didn't have a vision of a career, but everything he did was to survive and get by. Whatever job he could get, he took. He didn't let his pride get in his way.

After he moved to America, he found out many of the Jewish immigrants would meet in the Bronx on Southern Boulevard. Due to the big influx of Jews from Europe, the Jewish organizations held a dance every Saturday night for all the young refugees at the Ninety-Third Street Y. For many years he went to that hall and connected with people from all over Europe. He mostly associated with other refugees. His friends he met in the DP camps in Germany started going with him soon after. On Friday nights in the Bronx, he played cards with Herman, Big Joe, Little Joe, and others. An old lady let them play in her house and she used to serve them coffee and cake, provided they let her take 5 or 10 percent of the pot as payment.

"We all made minimum wage, but we played with big money," he joyfully reminisced.

When he first came to the United States, he walked to a synagogue for the high holidays. As part of his new life, he made small efforts to reincorporate Judaism. On the high holidays there is a service called yizkor held in memory of parents or children who have passed. When Poppy walked up to the shul, he was stopped and turned away at the door for not having a ticket. His blood boiled as he thought about not being able to honor his parents.

As he described this story, I heard the frustration in his voice. There was no way for him to know that high holiday tickets were commonplace in America. Turning away someone from a synagogue was unheard of in Munkacs. His single attempt at reconnecting was a failure. At that moment, he threw the religious part of Judaism out the door. He would still take off from work on the important holidays, but he didn't enter a temple again until he met my grandmother.

After about five years living and working in America, Bella introduced Poppy to my grandmother. Bella and my grandmother worked together as bookkeepers for Miller Factors. He wasn't in a rush to get married. He just wanted to move forward from the war and begin to live his life. There was never a thought in his mind to not marry or be associated with non-Jews. It wasn't too difficult for him because New York City had a big Jewish population, even larger than it is today.

"We met on Thanksgiving and by Christmas we were married. That's how the story goes." His smile grew almost bashfully as he described their less-than-fairytale love story.

They met and decided almost immediately they would spend the rest of their lives together. Over the years, I saw their relationship in a different light. They needed each other. After my grandfather stopped driving in his mid-eighties, my grandmother became the one who always sat behind the wheel. She was healthy enough physically to drive, but he directed her exactly where to turn in order to make it to their destination safe and sound. My family often joked that together they made a whole person. Poppy and Grandma would constantly kvetch and complain about each other, saying the other was driving them crazy.

"The day she wakes up and doesn't complain something's wrong, I'd worry about her," Poppy repeated anytime my grandmother made a fuss. There was always something new she wanted and would nag him about incessantly. The second she got it, she moved onto the next item on the agenda. The complaining was all a front. If my grandparents were separated for more than a half hour, they called asking when the other would come home.

Poppy's love was always conveyed that way. He was never one for many words, but he allowed his actions to speak for him.

Their wedding service was held in the basement of my grandma's parents' small railroad flat. It was a simple wedding without any special decorations, other than the chuppah, held by my grandmother's brothers and one of Poppy's friends. Beneath the canopy, my grandmother, only twenty-two in a ruffled and lacy off-white gown, married Poppy, who was thirty-three. The meal afterward was held in their dark, partially finished basement because it was the only room big enough to fit my grandmother's large immediate family.

Right after they got married, they found an apartment in Forest Hills, Queens. Moving to Forest Hills and starting their family was when Judaism became an active part of Poppy's daily life. My grandma grew up in a traditional Jewish household. Her family kept strictly kosher, and her grandmother only spoke Yiddish. Together, my grandmother and her grandmother went to synagogue every Saturday.

Grandma had a strong sense of connection to G-d and prayer. Poppy didn't really believe much in religion and his belief in G-d always remained skeptical. Their beliefs may have differed, but their priority was creating a Jewish house for their children and keeping tradition alive.

Poppy and Grandma played Jewish radio in the mornings. The house was kept kosher, except for a singular pan Poppy used for bacon. They became more active in Judaism by joining a shul, because, otherwise, he worried his family would disconnect from Judaism completely. Regardless of his own belief in religion, he knew he wanted his children to know they were Jewish. He wanted them to meet friends in shul. Judaism wasn't just a religion to him—it was a set of standards and values to live life by. He wanted to raise his children to be good people and have a proud connection to their history.

After my grandmother's mother passed away, my mom's family started hosting Passover at their house. She doesn't remember much about Passover before then but the one at her house was always a big event. Before Passover started, they emptied all the kitchen cabinets, washing them down from top to bottom. They relined them with either shelf-liner or contact paper to have them extra protected.

Next to the staircase was a hollow planter that looked like a white pony wall where they stored all the Passover dishes. It was built into the design of the house and Poppy put a countertop on top. This way, there was no schlepping the dishes up and down the stairs every year. They spent hours switching all of the non-Passover and Passover dishes. Every year Bella came to help prepare for Passover.

Bella's kids were much older than my mom and Penny. Their lives moved forward into marriage and adulthood while my mom was still a young girl. Bella then had increasingly more time to spend with my mom and her family. Passover was always a big event and Bella was the head chef with my mom and Penny as her sous-chefs. My mom loved cooking with Bella and all the tradition that came along with it. My grandfather worked so many hours, so he couldn't prepare. My grandmother also worked but she was never much help in the kitchen anyway. She stayed far away from cooking, usually because she only made two dishes: luchen kugel or meatloaf "surprise." Only the luchen kugel was edible.

Bella, on the other hand, was unbelievable in the kitchen. She was an incredible chef and baker, making every Jewish pastry from scratch.

"We used to make rugelach and a poppy seed pastry roll, similar to a babka. Bella took the dough and spread it across the entire counter. Then, she would lay the poppy seed filling all over it, roll the pastry up, and bake it. Bella came up with different fillings and creations. My favorite was poppy seed or nuts with cinnamon and sugar." As my mom described baking with Bella in her parents' kitchen, she spoke with the same affection I felt when talking about baking with her.

Bella always made my mom feel special. Occasionally she would spend the weekend with her and they shared alone time together. This relationship was unlike anything she had with any of her other aunts.

Eventually, after spending so much time cooking together, they got to a point where everyone knew their job and each other's movements. Mom's job was to peel carrots and potatoes, which became my job growing up. She peels faster than a machine ever could and with fewer mistakes. Instead of having a big party for Penny's sweet sixteen, Poppy realized with that money he could finish their basement. They lived in a row house, so the basement was long and narrow. Once the basement was finished, he put a small utility kitchen down there that became their Passover kitchen. It was a refrigerator, a little countertop, a sink, and a small stove.

"We always held Passover seders in the basement in Bayonne. The first night we had some of your grandmother's six brothers and sisters. They didn't all come the first night, but we always had at least twenty people. We used whatever we could as chairs," Poppy reminisced. In the basement, there were old pleather brown couches my mom, Penny, Donna, and the other kids sat on. The couches were so old and worn out that, when someone sat in them, they sank. The kids sat on the couch and had their heads at table level because the couch was so low down. Most of them wouldn't get up the entire night because it was too much effort to pull themselves out of the black hole that was the couch.

The table and seating lined her family from one end of the basement to the other. Elly, my grandmother's father, led the seder. He was strict, even telling Poppy to be quiet. Unlike my family growing up, Elly led the seder as a monologue, without people taking turns reading. The only exception was the four questions for which the youngest at the seder, usually Donna, was permitted to recite. Then, Elly would continue. He read the English, then the Hebrew, giving his interpretations in between like he was some kind of preacher. One of the kids always got up to go to the bathroom and bring food back downstairs in secret. They passed it underneath the table so they wouldn't starve during the seder that went on for hours.

One year, someone had the idea to take out some of the pages from Elly's Haggadah because they couldn't stand another year of the never-ending seder. Somehow, my mom's

Uncle Stanley got that Haggadah instead of Elly and spent the whole night confused because he was missing pages.

Another year, my mom's Aunt Marcia was sitting all the way at the far end of the table smoking cigarettes. When my grandfather asked her to stop, she responded, "I don't care we're inside. I'll do it anyway." The first night was always a production with strong personalities and way too much food.

The second night was always smaller. Elly was there both nights, but my mom's aunts and uncles wouldn't always stay. With usually only eighteen people, the seder was calmer with less craziness than the first night. Bella was there the whole time, usually sleeping over. Sometimes her kids came too.

Passover was always my mom's favorite holiday. It was the only time during the year her entire family came together. Rosh Hashanah and Yom Kippur were always just the four of them and sometimes Bella. Even for Thanksgiving they didn't all come together as a family event. It was only ever Passover.

While Passover remained the big Jewish event of the year, there were more regular reminders of culture and history. Every Friday night they had Shabbat dinner together because Poppy's family growing up had Shabbat dinner every Friday. It was his way of connecting and remembering them. After dinner, he then played cards with his friends. Even after moving from Queens to Bayonne in December of 1971, his weekly card games continued with a new group of survivors in his new town. The old friends, Big Joe, Little Joe, and Herman, continued to see each other all the time. Those men were his best friends, his brothers, and they kept those friendships until the day they died.

For years, Poppy saved up money and even took a personal loan to bring Sidi, Imre, and their daughter to America before the Hungarian Revolution in 1956. He sent Bella's husband to bring them over but didn't know Sidi just had a son. There wasn't enough money to bring four of them over, so Sidi and her family remained in Budapest. "Every Sunday after that, I called Sidi in Hungary. It was fifteen dollars to call internationally for only a few minutes. Back then, it was a lot of money." Every cent was worth it for Poppy to hear his sister's voice.

Bayonne is a city with little delis and mom-and-pop convenience stores on every other corner. When my mom was about five years old, Poppy heard the small grocery store on the corner was owned by a man from Munkacs. Poppy walked around the corner to the store and introduced himself to the man behind the counter. Harry Herman was from Munkacs and closer in age to Poppy's brother, Yoshka. Poppy didn't know him well because Harry's family was from the more religious part of town.

"After I introduced myself, he told me he knew my brother from the labor camps in Yugoslavia. He told me about the day my brother was killed. They were marching back to Germany and a solider was playing with his gun. My brother got shot in the leg. He couldn't walk, so the soldier shot him completely. That was how I found out my brother died." As Poppy spoke, he looked out the window.

From that point on, Poppy and Harry became close friends. Harry owned and operated the store with his wife, Helen, and his sister-in-law. They used to call Poppy *kisci*, which is Hungarian for "little" because he was younger than them. On weekends, Poppy went to the store and talked to him, sometimes helping him stock shelves.

"When Harry's son, Jeff, was little, he got dragged to the store to help stock shelves. The store opened at 5:30 and we were there even earlier. Jeff was so tired he would fall asleep in his coat when he was supposed to be working."

Whenever my mom or Penny needed anything from fresh American cheese to meat, they went to Harry's store. In the front of the store there were penny candies. There was a big container of Swedish fish and little brown bags to put the candies in. Sometimes, Helen took one of the brown paper penny candy bags and filled it with Swedish fish, saying kindly to my mom, "Don't tell your parents." Poppy didn't have to worry about leaving my mom and aunt with money, and he rarely did because they always knew they had a place to go. Harry kept a tab and Poppy went in over the weekend and paid whatever the family owed him for the week.

Once Penny went to high school, my eight-year-old mom came home for lunch alone every day. As a third-grader, she sometimes forgot her keys and locked herself out of the house. When this happened, she went to Harry's store because she had nowhere else to go. In the back of the store, Harry had a butcher block from cutting meat. He covered the butcher block with cardboard and took a milk crate with a cushion tied to it, making her a little seat and a sandwich for lunch. She could taste the freshness of their kaiser rolls in each bite. My mom loved going there. Every once in a while, when she didn't feel like being by herself, she went over to the store and said she locked herself out just to have a good sandwich and some company.

Harry and Helen became part of the village that raised my mom.

Harry's family owned a series of these small deli convenience stores. His brother-in-law decided to scale back a little, so they sold the store closest to my mom's house. The other store was across town and not close enough to walk to. Poppy went there occasionally but he wouldn't see the Hermans as much. Then, they sold that store too and Poppy lost touch with them.

Years later, Penny's daughter was attending Solomon Schechter Day School. They had a grandparents' shabbaton, so naturally Poppy and Grandma went.

"Your grandmother was sitting there and looking at the woman next to her. She was confused, which is normal, but she knew the woman. It was Helen."

By a twist of fate, Helen's and Harry's granddaughter was in Schechter. The Hermans were still living up north in Maplewood and my grandparents were still in Bayonne. Once they reconnected, they picked up where they left off, speaking regularly and always sharing stories about their grandchildren. Soon after, Poppy and Grandma moved to Monroe and Helen and Harry were looking to move to Monroe too. They were interested in a different development and eventually moved to the development across the street, Concordia.

A few years later, Harry's son Jeff bought a house three doors down from my family in East Brunswick. Years later, their family was still part of our little village. Our intertwined paths continued through the generations.

On Passover, Helen made a delicious nut cake my grandparents adored. It was always at least nine inches high and incredibly moist. Eventually, my mom asked Helen for the recipe, although through all the years she could never replicate the signature height. When Jeff and his wife, Elise, first moved to East Brunswick, my mom made multiple nut cakes for Passover.

"I walked over to Jeff's house to give him one. I told him I knew it wouldn't be as good as his mother's. Funny enough, he told me he never liked the nut cake and couldn't believe we still made it. That cake was my family's favorite Passover recipe." My mom smiled softly as she spoke.

Helen and Harry held a special place in my mom's heart from her time growing up in Bayonne. Through all his loss, Poppy created a new family both by blood and by choice. The Hermans were the family Poppy chose.

CHAPTER FOURTEEN

POPPY'S LESSONS

———

Family was the center of Poppy's universe, whether it was family in which he was born, married, or by choice. It was always the guiding tenant of his life. Because of his profound impact on everyone around him, Poppy's life lessons have become the set of standards I use to create a fulfilling and happy life.

THE MOST IMPORTANT THING IN LIFE IS FAMILY

Poppy's family was broken up, and for many years he couldn't find his way because he was on his own. His family helped him gain the strength and direction to create his future.

Poppy's immense pride in his family led him to help them, no matter what. My mother told me a story about when Poppy's cousin Iszo came to America. Iszo was the cousin that made a deal to transport their possessions from Munkacs. His sister was an incredible seamstress who worked day in and day out. Since she worked out of the house, she worked at all hours of the day, running herself into the ground with no breaks. When she tried to limit her work intake, people nearby begged her to take their items, and who was she to say no?

She and her husband were very close to Bella because they lived near each other. Iszo stayed back in Munkacs after the war. Iszo and his sister wrote letters back and forth because she was trying to find a way to get him out of the Soviet Union. Jews were especially in danger there. Amid their correspondence, she suffered a fatal heart attack.

Bella's daughter Linda and her fiancé went over to the house to help the two young daughters and grieving husband for a few months. She was out of high school and soon after got married. During the commotion at their home, no one looked at the letters Iszo sent from Hungary. Even if they did, it wouldn't be much help, since his sister was the only one who spoke Hungarian.

In the middle of the night, the phone in Poppy's small Queens apartment began to ring. He awoke and in a tired haze picked up the phone.

"I heard on the phone, 'It's Iszo. We're at the airport but my sister isn't here. Can you come get us?' He said he looked through the phone books for our last name because it was unique. I had to tell him his sister just had a heart attack and couldn't pick him up. I didn't know if I was dreaming or what. So, I did the only thing I could do."

The alarm of his family being stranded at John F. Kennedy airport gave him a jolt of energy better than his morning coffee. Knowing his sedan was far too small to fit a family of four and their belongings necessary to start a new life, he called Linda to enlist her help. Poppy hadn't seen or spoken to Iszo in nearly fifteen years and Linda had probably never met or heard of him, but there they were, trekking across New York in the middle of the night to help their family begin a new life. As they arrived at the airport, they loaded the luggage into one car and the people into another. It was like they left Anatevka and brought all their possessions with them. There was no animosity of the trials and tribulations of family items lost in Eastern Europe. There was only hope and optimism for the new life that lay ahead of their family. Arriving back at his two-bedroom apartment in Queens, it was evident the space was not meant for a family of four, let alone two families plus a newlywed couple. My mom and Penny, at the time, were ages three and nine, respectively. They awoke early the next morning, seeing the faint whisper of the sun rising over the New York city skyline. They were confused and overwhelmed waking up in their parents' bed to a house full of strangers. The already cramped space was full of suitcases and people, making it difficult to determine where the floor was.

For the next few weeks, Poppy and Grandma spent all their time looking for ways to help Iszo and his family establish themselves as a desperate attempt to get them out of their apartment and onto their own path. They found them a garden apartment in a nearby building and Grandma enrolled their son in the junior high school. She even introduced their daughter to the butcher's nephew. They now have three children and countless grandchildren.

There was little reason for Poppy to have helped Iszo and his family. They hadn't spoken for years, and yet he took on the responsibility to set them up with life in America. He could have held grudges from when his possessions were never returned after Iszo organized the transport, but he didn't. Instead, Poppy focused on helping his family begin their new life in the face of adversity and grief.

"The most important thing in life is the family. With the family, everyone is different. You treat people the way they are. Don't change a guy who likes one thing to like another thing. You have to compromise somewhere. It's like telling Ben to take off those crazy pants."

For as long as I can remember, my brother has been an interesting character. It became the most apparent late in high school when he dyed his hair bright purple one summer and lime green the next. As he explored himself further, his clothing changed. He wore vibrant patterns and pants with lots of zippers. When other people stared at the strange clothes Ben wore, Poppy smiled. He sometimes joked asking Ben if he could get a pair in his size. There was no judgment, only acceptance and pride that Ben was comfortable in his own skin. There was no reason to ask him to dress like everyone else because he wasn't like everyone else. Clothing can be a form of self-expression and Poppy was happy to see Ben feeling comfortable in his own skin.

No matter who the person in the family was, Poppy supported and cared for them. He supported them to achieve as much as they could. The clearest example of that can be seen in my mom's cousin Donna. She was one of Poppy's nieces, but she and her sister became almost like additional children to my grandparents. Her parents were always out and about, so frequently she was left on my grandparents' steps in Bayonne, waiting for them to come home from work on a Friday night.

Even though they usually didn't know when she was coming, they welcomed her into their home with open arms and she felt like they wanted her there. When she was little, Poppy always came over and sat with her. Even if they didn't say anything, his presence comforted her. He handed her an Andes mint behind everyone's back as a little treat to hopefully lighten her mood. Every time she sees Andes mints, she still thinks of him.

When she graduated high school, Poppy encouraged her to go to college and get away. "Her father claimed she wasn't college material. She wasn't such a great student in high school. I told him she needed to experience life away from home to succeed." He believed in her even when she couldn't believe in herself.

THE IMPORTANCE OF HONESTY AND RESPECTING YOUR CHILDREN

From a young age, honesty and respect were critical elements in Poppy's life. When he was a teenager during the beginning of the war, he got a job working at the hat-checking business at the nightclub. When he returned home from work, he left the money he earned on the table to help support his family. No one ever asked him how much money he made that night; they just expected him to help contribute to the family.

"Most of the things in life you learn from somebody," he said. This honesty and respect from his parents led the way for how he raised his children. Poppy didn't need to tell Penny or Mom directly if business was going well or not, but he also wouldn't censor himself from talking about business in their presence. He spoke to his daughters like adults, giving them their own responsibilities around the house. They knew where he kept extra money for necessities and were expected to tell him when and why they took it. He then replaced it and the cycle continued. Giving his children responsibilities and respecting them led to the two strong and self-sufficient women I know now.

The combination of love, respect, and support allowed his children to follow their passions. This led to respect and support going both ways. He encouraged them to challenge themselves and pursue their passions. Everything his children do is to make him proud, even until today. Part of my perpetual guilt is because of this. Every decision I make is like having a little voice in the back of my head asking, *Would Poppy be proud of you for this?*

THE IMPORTANCE OF MOVING FORWARD
AND NOT TAKING LIFE TOO SERIOUSLY

Many of the people who came as refugees from Europe were hardworking people. Like Poppy, they built themselves up to become middle-class citizens in the United States. Some even went on to become very successful and make more than a decent living. The reason for success was, in part, due to there being no fear of failure. So much was already taken from survivors that losing money or a job wasn't the end of the world. The people who survived the Holocaust had to be strong, both mentally and physically. Poppy moved on from the tragedies in his life and the trauma of losing his family in order to create his new family.

"So, how did you move past what happened to you?" I prodded.

"If you want to live, you don't take everything 100 percent seriously."

He was a man with few regrets. There is no time in our short lives to waste dwelling on things we cannot change. Poppy always said the phrase, "It's your America." He believed the United States did a lot of good for Jews and for him. It was full of freedom and opportunity, so he felt immense appreciation. Even though he tried to move forward in his life, he still thought about his parents every day. Some way or another, he was reminded of them, their home, and the life that was ripped away. If he could tell or show his parents anything, he would want them to see he had a nice family.

He came to America without a big education or any money, but he made a decent living and brought up his family nicely. "What else can you ask for out of life?"

We are the sum of our experiences. Not just the sum of our own personal experiences but also of the collective experiences of the generations preceding us. We carry on that legacy, both the good and the bad. The most important thing I have learned throughout this journey is not what the bad things that happened to us are, but rather how we choose to let those negative experiences influence and affect the people we are now.

We are not defined by the negative things that happen to us. We are not our failures and we are so much more than our struggles. If you choose to live in the past, you will live the rest of your life as a victim. The way we allow our negative experiences to determine our future is how we define our lives.

RECIPES

———

PEASANT SOUP

This recipe fits in a six- to eight-quart soup pot and can be modified to make larger or smaller quantities. To make this soup vegetarian, substitute vegetable broth or bullion for the flanken. Feel free to adjust the amount of flanken based on how meaty you would like the flavor to be. Poppy usually used smaller amounts.

INGREDIENTS

- 1 cup barley
- 1 cup split green peas
- 1 cup split yellow peas
- 1 cup lima beans
- One medium onion, peeled
- One medium potato
- One medium grated carrot
- 1 lb. flanken (a piece of short rib soup beef)
- Salt and pepper

INSTRUCTIONS

1. Soak equal parts barley, beans, and peas overnight in water.
2. Strain water from soaked legumes.
3. In a large heavy soup pot, add barley, beans, yellow peas, green peas, flanken, whole onion, and grated carrot.
4. Fill pot with water.
5. Bring to a boil and lower to a simmer, cover.
6. Cook for about three hours.
7. Cut a potato into quarter inch thick slices.
8. Add potato to soup.
9. Cook until everything is soft, usually about four to five hours in total.
10. Add water if soup appears too thick.
11. Add salt and pepper to taste before serving.

GOULASH

Goulash can be served either as a stew or a soup. To make as more of a soup, add water and potatoes until the desired consistency is reached.

INGREDIENTS

- 1 medium onion
- 1 medium carrot, peeled and grated
- 1 tsp. fresh garlic or garlic powder
- 1/4 tsp. pepper
- 1/2 tsp. paprika
- One tomato (vine or Roma)
- 1–1.5 pounds beef stew meat
- 2 tbsp. vegetable oil
- Salt (to taste)
- *Optional: water and peeled and cubed potatoes*

INSTRUCTIONS

1. Heat oil in a heavy stew pot to prevent burning and charring.
2. Add onions and sauté until translucent.
3. Add garlic and carrots, mixing together.
4. Mix in paprika and pepper.
5. Add beef cubes and brown on a medium or medium-high flame.
6. Once the meat is browned (approximately five minutes), lower the flame, throw in chopped tomato, cover, and cook for two to two and a half hours on a low flame, checking and mixing periodically. It should produce a lot of gravy or sauce.
7. In the last fifteen minutes, taste and season to taste with salt, pepper, and paprika.
8. To serve as more of a soup, add water and seasoning into the pan in the last ten minutes and add cubed potatoes into the pan. Allow them to cook in the sauce, covered, until soft.

CHICKEN PAPRIKASH

Growing up, my grandfather's family kept kosher. They modified the traditional recipe by making it more like goulash. The recipes are nearly identical, excluding the variations to make it soup as opposed to stew.

INGREDIENTS

- One medium onion
- One medium carrot, peeled and grated
- 1 tsp. fresh garlic or garlic powder
- 1/4 tsp. pepper
- 1/2 tsp. paprika
- One tomato (vine or Roma)
- 1-1.5 lbs. chicken parts
- 2 tbsp. vegetable oil
- Salt (to taste)

INSTRUCTIONS

1. Heat oil in a heavy stew pot to prevent burning and charring.
2. Add onions and sauté until translucent.
3. Add garlic and carrots, mixing together.
4. Mix in paprika and pepper.
5. Add chicken and brown on a medium or medium-high flame.
6. Once the meat is browned (approximately five minutes), lower the flame, throw in chopped tomato, cover, and cook for two to two and a half hours on a low flame, checking and mixing periodically. It should produce a lot of gravy or sauce.
7. In the last fifteen minutes, taste and season to taste with salt, pepper, and paprika.

LECSO

Growing up, Poppy used to make lecso with chopped hot dogs, but traditionally the dish is made with sliced sausage. Over the years we have substituted different types of sausages and they all add their own flavor to the dish. To make this dish vegetarian, exclude the sausage or use a vegetarian substitute.

INGREDIENTS

- One large onion
- Two medium-to-large peppers
- Approximately 2 tbsp. fresh chopped garlic
- 2–3 tbsp. vegetable oil
- 2 tsp. hot paprika
- 2 tsp. sweet paprika paste, csemege
- 1/4 tsp. pepper
- 28 oz. can crushed tomatoes
- Sliced sausage or hot dogs
- Salt (to taste)
- *Optional: eggs to poach on top*

INSTRUCTIONS

1. Cut onions in half and then into thin slivers.
2. Cut peppers into slices about 1/4 inch to 1/2 inch thick.
3. Heat vegetable oil in a pan.
4. Once warm, add onions, garlic, and peppers and sauté until onions are translucent.
5. Add paprika and pepper.
6. Add twenty-eight oz. can crushed tomatoes
7. Lower the temperature and let simmer, covered, for at least an hour.
8. Add the meat and cook for at least another thirty minutes.
9. Crack eggs on top and poach.
10. Add salt and pepper to taste before serving.

HUNGARIAN MEATBALLS

INGREDIENTS

- 1.5 lbs. ground beef
- Two eggs
- Dash of pepper
- 1/2 tsp. paprika
- 1/2 tsp. garlic powder
- 1/2 cup par cooked rice
- 2 lb. bag of sauerkraut, strained
- Two 28 oz. cans of crushed tomatoes (can be substituted for tomato sauce)

INSTRUCTIONS

1. Preheat the oven to 350 degrees.
2. Mix meat, eggs, pepper, paprika, and garlic powder until fully combined.
3. To prepare the rice, cook but not until it is too fluffy. When the meatballs cook, the rice absorbs liquid and expands, making the meatballs fluffy. Add the rice, mixing until the meat mixture holds together without sticking to the bottom or sides of the bowl.
4. Mix half of the tomato sauce with about half of the sauerkraut, add garlic powder, paprika, and pepper, mixing until combined.
5. Add the tomato mixture to the bottom of a deep and heavy baking pan (about 13x9 in).
6. Make golf-ball-sized meatballs and place into the pan so there is one flat layer, if possible.
7. Make the same tomato mixture with the other half of tomatoes, sauerkraut, and seasoning.
8. Cover the meatballs with sauce, ensuring all meatballs are covered.

9. Traditionally, Hungarian meatballs are made in a Dutch oven on the stovetop over a low flame. Mix constantly until meatballs are cooked through (at least one hour).

10. Alternative baking method is to put meatballs in the oven on the middle rack, cover, and bake for an hour to an hour and a half, mixing periodically to check on it after about forty-five minutes to one hour.

BRISKET

INGREDIENTS

- Three 16 oz. cans of whole cranberry sauce
- Two packages of Goodman's onion soup mix
- 5 lbs. brisket

INSTRUCTIONS

1. Preheat the oven to 325 degrees.
2. Place whole brisket in a heavy baking pan, big enough the brisket can fit comfortably but without so much space that the brisket is lost in the pan. If the pan is too big the sauce created will not soak into the meat, which adds flavor and moisture.
3. Pour onion soup mix on top of the brisket.
4. Take the cans of cranberry sauce, pouring on top and around the brisket.
5. Cover the brisket with aluminum foil.
6. Bake for two and a half to three hours.
7. Remove brisket from oven.
8. Take the brisket out of the pan and place it on a cutting board to cool.
9. Once the brisket is cooled enough that it is warm but not hot to the touch, slice it against the grain at your own discretion for thickness.
10. Once the brisket is sliced, carefully place it back into the sauce as one brisket. Cover and place it in the refrigerator at least overnight, but preferably for one to two days.
11. Take out of the refrigerator and put in the oven for another one and a half to two hours, covered, to finish cooking and leave it covered until ready to serve.

POPPY'S MAMALIGA

Mamaliga is an Eastern European hot cereal. It can be made with any cheese available. Traditionally it is made with goat cheese, but I prefer to make it with cheddar. This is the type of recipe where measuring cheese with your heart is better than putting it in a measuring cup.

INGREDIENTS (PER ONE SERVING)
- 1/4 cup cornmeal
- 1 cup milk (or water)
- 1/4–1/2 cup cheese
- Salt (to taste)
- Sour cream

INSTRUCTIONS
1. Mix together cornmeal, milk, and salt in a saucepan.
2. Cook over medium heat for approximately two minutes, stirring constantly.
3. Add in cheese, stirring until melted and combined.
4. Cover saucepan, lower heat to a low setting, and let sit for seven to eight minutes.
5. Uncover pan and mix to ensure thick, creamy consistency.
6. Transfer to a bowl and serve with sour cream on top.

KLUTZKAHS

INGREDIENTS

- 1 lb. potatoes
- 2 ½ cups flour
- 1 tbsp. seltzer
- Two eggs
- 1 tsp. salt
- 1/4 tsp. pepper
- 1/2 tsp. paprika
- 2/3 cup plain breadcrumbs
- 1 tbsp. olive oil (or other vegetable oil)

INSTRUCTIONS

1. Peel and cut the potatoes into cubes, approximately eight to ten pieces (depending on the size of the potatoes).
2. Boil water and some salt in a large pot.
3. Add the potatoes once the water has reached a rolling boil.
4. Cook potatoes for approximately fifteen minutes until they are soft and can be pierced by a fork easily.
5. Put potatoes into a food mill, mixing until all potatoes have been processed through the mill.
6. Let potatoes sit for approximately twenty minutes until room temperature.
7. Add flour, salt, pepper, and paprika, mixing by hand until a dough starts to form.
8. Add eggs and seltzer, mixing until combined.
9. Add additional flour until dough is soft and barely sticks to a finger if inserted into the dough.
10. Place dough in refrigerator for approximately one hour to cool and firm.
11. Boil water and some salt in a large pot (or two).
12. Take dough out of the fridge and place some on a wet or floured wooden cutting board.

13. With a long straight knife, flatten dough slightly.
14. Stick the knife into the boiling water, then cut approximately two-inch pieces on a diagonal angle, letting the knife roll under the dough.
15. Slice piece of dough into the boiling water, sticking the knife in to prevent sticking, continuing this process for the remaining dough.
16. Boil for approximately eight to ten minutes, depending on size of the dumplings, until insides are a soft texture.
17. Strain dumplings and run over with cold water.
18. In a large skillet, sauté breadcrumbs in olive oil until golden brown.
19. This may require dividing the klutzkahs into two batches. Add klutzkahs to breadcrumbs and mix on a medium heat until evenly coated.
20. Remove klutzkahs from pan and eat or reheat later in a frying pan or oven to get crispy.
21. Serve plain, underneath sauce, from lecso, goulash, or paprikash, or with cinnamon and sugar.

FLAKES

INGREDIENTS

- 1 tbsp. vegetable oil
- 12 oz. package egg noo-
  dle flakes
- 2 cups hot water

- 1 tsp. paprika
- 1 tsp. salt
- 1/2 tsp. pepper

INSTRUCTIONS

1. Put flakes and vegetable into a saucepan and sauté over medium/medium high heat until golden brown.
2. Add two cups of hot water.
3. Add salt, pepper, and paprika.
4. Mix, bring to a simmer, and cover.
5. Cook until all water is absorbed and flakes are soft (approximately ten minutes).
6. If water is absorbed but flakes are still hard, add more water.

FARFEL KUGEL

INGREDIENTS

- 3 cups matzah farfel
- Five separated eggs
- 1 tsp. salt
- 1/4 cup sugar
- 1/4 cup melted butter (or margarine)
- 2 cups applesauce
- 3/4 cup crushed pineapple (drained)
- 1/2 tsp. cinnamon

INSTRUCTIONS

1. Preheat oven to 325 degrees.
2. Grease a 9x9 baking pan.
3. Soften matzah farfel with water.
4. Beat egg yolks, salt, sugar, cinnamon, and butter/margarine.
5. Add mixture to the softened matzah farfel.
6. Add in pineapple and applesauce.
7. In a separate bowl, beat egg whites to soft peaks.
8. Fold the whites into the mixture.
9. Bake for forty-five to sixty minutes until there is a slight jiggle when you agitate the pan.

GRANDMA ESTHER'S LUCHEN (NOODLE) KUGEL

INGREDIENTS

- 1 package 16 oz. wide egg noodles
- Four eggs
- 1/4 cup of sugar (more or less to taste)
- Cinnamon
- Five apples, peeled
- Handful of raisins

INSTRUCTIONS

1. Bring a pot of water to a boil and cook egg noodles until soft. Then rinse with cold water.
2. Grate peeled apples with a large box grater or put into a food processor until it is in fine pieces.
3. Mix eggs, sugar, cinnamon, raisins, and grated apples into cooked egg noodles.
4. Bake at 350, covered for one and a half hours. Take off covering and allow to cook uncovered until crispy on top and ready to serve.

HELEN'S NUT CAKE

INGREDIENTS

- Twelve eggs (separate yolks from whites)
- 1 3/4 cup sugar
- 1 cup matzah cake meal
- 8 oz. ground walnuts
- 1/3 cup orange juice
- 1/2 lemon zest and juice

INSTRUCTIONS

1. Preheat oven to 350 degrees.
2. Grease a deep Bundt pan.
3. Beat together sugar and whites until stiff peaks.
4. Beat yolks in a separate bowl.
5. Fold yolks into whites and add cake meal, walnuts, orange juice, and lemon.
6. Bake for one hour and ten minutes.
7. After removing from oven, turn pan upside down and let cool completely before removing from pan.

HAMANTASCHEN

INGREDIENTS

Dough:

- Four eggs
- 3/4 cup oil
- 1 1/4 cup sugar
- 1 1/2 tsp. salt
- 4 tsp. baking powder
- 5+ cups of flour
- 1 orange juice and rind (or 2–4 tbsp. of orange juice)
- 1 tsp. vanilla extract

Filling

- Jam, poppy seed, chocolate chips, prune preserves, etc.

INSTRUCTIONS

1. Beat eggs, oil, sugar, vanilla, and orange in mixer until well combined.
2. Add salt and baking powder.
3. Add in five cups flour (one cup at a time) until a soft dough forms.
4. Wrap dough in plastic wrap and put into the refrigerator for at least one hour to rest.
5. Preheat oven to 350 degrees.
6. Line cookie sheets with parchment paper.
7. Lightly flour counter and roll out dough until 1/4 inch thick.
8. Using a glass or round cookie cutter, create circles.
9. Add filling to the center, then wet outside of the dough circle by dipping a finger in a glass of water and running it along the perimeter.
10. Pinch together corners to make a triangle shape.
11. Bake on lined cookie sheets for approximately twenty minutes or until the edges start to become golden brown.

ACKNOWLEDGMENTS

———

Writing this story was a long and difficult process. The day after I finished my first draft, Poppy passed away and I almost decided not to continue. To my family and friends who pushed me to keep going, this would not have been possible without you. To each and every person who read this book from beginning to end, thank you for helping to carry on my grandfather's legacy.

I am forever grateful to all my family and friends who encouraged my writing process and contributed to this book. Thank you to everyone who allowed me to share their stories.

Thank you to my parents, Joannie and Jerry, and my brother, Ben, for listening to me talk incessantly about this book since before I started writing it. You are all superheroes and I look up to you more than you know. There is still much I have to learn from you.

To Grandma Esther for answering all my questions and for sitting at the table for hours with me and Poppy every weekend. I hope when I'm eighty, my husband is still walking to the kitchen in the middle of the night to get me that piece of chocolate.

Thank you, Poppa, for your love and support throughout this journey. You always knew how to make me laugh even when I wanted to cry.

To Bubba, for sharing your love of literature and storytelling with me. You were such an integral part of my love of reading and writing. Thank you for your encouragement during this process. I wish you could have been here to see the finished product. I miss you every day.

To Harrison, for forcing me to sit down and do the work, even when it was easier not to. I am endlessly grateful for you and am so lucky to have had you by my side every step of the way.

A heartfelt thank you to the team at New Degree Press for their hard work to support me on my publishing journey, including Natalie Bailey, Joanna Hatzikazakis, Brian Bies, Bosko Maksimovic, Jess Nielsen Beach, and Caitlin Mathey. An extra special thank you to Benay Stein for testing out the recipes while we worked together. I need to thank Eric Koester of the Creator Institute and Georgetown University for his encouragement and coaching.

I also want to thank the very generous group of individuals who purchased a copy of this book during the pre-sale. You are the ones who made the publication of this story possible. Thank you for making an investment in my story and my writing.

Aaron, Sarah, and Alexia Friedman

Adam Jucovic

Adam Rosen

Adrienne Frank

Alan Shindelman

Alexis Ciccone

Ali Overmyer

Andrea Kaufman

Andrew Albero

Anne Kroll

Arlene and Paul Rosenberg

Aron Finkelstein

Barbara Snepar

Ben Weinfeld

Beth G. Finkle

Betty Robalino

Bonnie and Gary Kudwitt

Bosco Kudwitt

Brian Weir-Harden

Butch Seltzer

Candace Stabile

Cara E. Turcich

Carina Weber

Cindy and Rick Rollman

Cindy Skaar

Colleen and Jeffrey
Schwimmer

Cynthia Engel

Danielle Eiger

David Pryluck

David Rosenstein

David Strinkovsky

Deirdre Montel

Dina Broydo

Donna, John,
and Sofia Marchetta

Drew Walcott

Elizabeth Schwimmer

Emanuel Zur

Emily Bravman

Emily Charniga

Emily Goslin

Emma Rothenberg

Eric Koester

Eric Ravens

Erik and Liz Kaplansky

Erika Sawicki

Esther Jucowics

Gabriel Charney

Garland Frame Middleton

Gina Lauricella

Gina Lerner

Griffin Brightbill

Harrison Kudwitt

Hayley and Alan Migdal

Heaven's Pantry LLC

Hy & Marcia Pryluck

Jack Roscoe

Jacob Orgel

Jaime Martin Ko Atilano

Janey Huber

Janis Davisson

Jason Recht

Jeff Pryluck

Jeffrey and Elyse Herman

Jerry and Joannie Weinfeld

Jillian Dorsey
and Evan Angstreich

Jocelyn Shepke

Jodi and Steve Feldstein

Joseph Burns

Josh Lasky

Joshua Montel

Julia Mattson

Juliet Volosin

June Miller

Katelyn Wilbur

Katie Kincaid

Katie Murnane

Kelly and Allan Berman

Kira Soloff

Kristina Bonfiglio

Lauren Goldstein

Linda Fellen
and Ben Gottesman

Linda and Sam Friedman

Logan Dill

Marcie Beth Levinson

Marty and Mindy
Angstreich

Maya Romanchuk

Melissa Levinson

Michael McDonald

Mikayla Talmud

Mike Shannon

Missy, Mitch, Rachel,
and Ryan Codkind

Natalie Corson

Natalie Turner

Natalie Valenzuela

Nathan Bishop

Nick Saglimbeni

Paul, Roberta, Zachary, and Heather Solomon

Penny and Brad Cohen

Poppa

Rachel Cohen

Rachel Degutz

Rachel Moskowitz

Rachel Salem

Rachel Weinthal

Randy and Lisa Cohen

Rebecca Kosher

Rebecca Roberts

Robert Bringardner

Robert Bryson

Robert Calo

Robert Zuckerman

Russell Caratenuto

Samuel Roth

Sandy and Elyssa Resnick

Sara Benz

Sara Fleischer

Sara Friedman

Scott, Tara, Sarah, and Jane Weinfeld

Serena Young

Seth Gruhin

Susan Lasky

Sydney Hyde

Tanya Kuzmina

The Becker Family

The Benson Family

The Bier Family

The Brenner Family

The Chananie Family

The Folz Family

The Footerman Family

The Greenspan Family

The Kroll Family

The Kuba Family

The Lenner Family

The Lowe Family

The Nargund Family

The Pelletier Family

The Steiner Family

The Susskind Family

The Wasserman Family

The Weinstein Family

Tracey and Evan Levy

Rabbi Lisa Malik and the
entire Malik-Wyner Family

Vanessa Amaturo

Vanessa Masick

Zoe Levitt

APPENDIX

CHAPTER THREE

Holocaust Matters. "Fünfteichen Camp–Overview." Accessed June 2022. https://www.holocaustmatters.org/fnfteichen-camp-overview/.

CHAPTER ELEVEN

Bader, Heather, Linda Bierer, Elisabeth Binder, Nikolaos Daskalakis, Torsten Klengel, Amy Lehrner, Iouri Makotkine, Nadine Provençal, Tobias Wiechmann, and Rachel Yehuda. "Intergenerational Effects of Maternal Holocaust Exposure on FKBP5 Methylation." *American Journal of Psychiatry* 171, no. 8 (2014). https://doi.org/10.1176/appi.ajp.2019.19060618.

DeAngelis, Tori. "The Legacy of Trauma." *American Psychological Association* 50, no. 2 (February 2019): 36. https://www.apa.org/monitor/2019/02/legacy-trauma.

Sigal, John, Vincenzo Dinicola, and Michael Buonvino. "Grandchildren of Survivors: Can Negative Effects of Prolonged Exposure to Excessive Stress Be Observed Two Generations Later?" *The Canadian Journal of Psychology* 33, no. 3 (1988). https://doi.org/10.1177/070674378803300309.

CPSIA information can be obtained
at www.ICGtesting.com
Printed in the USA
LVHW100205221122
733777LV00006B/434